Bayside Impressions

MARYLAND'S EASTERN SHORE AND THE CHESAPEAKE BAY

Bayside Impressions

Maryland's Eastern Shore and the Chesapeake Bay

WATERCOLORS BY JAMES DRAKE IAMS, A. W. S.

TEXT BY WILLIAM L. THOMPSON

TIDEWATER PUBLISHERS : CENTREVILLE, MARYLAND

Library of Congress Cataloging in Publication Data

Iams, James Drake, 1927-   Bayside impressions.

1. Iams, James Drake, 1927-   2. Eastern Shore (Md. and Va.) in art.   3. Chesapeake Bay (Md. and Va.) in art.   4. Water-color painting—Technique.   I. Thompson, William L., 1948-   II. Title.
ND1839.I23A4   1984   759.13   83-40047
ISBN 0-87033-304-6
ISBN 0-87033-321-6 (Ltd)

Manufactured in the United States of America
First edition

*To those regional artists
who appreciate and capture the scenic beauty
of the Chesapeake Bay country*

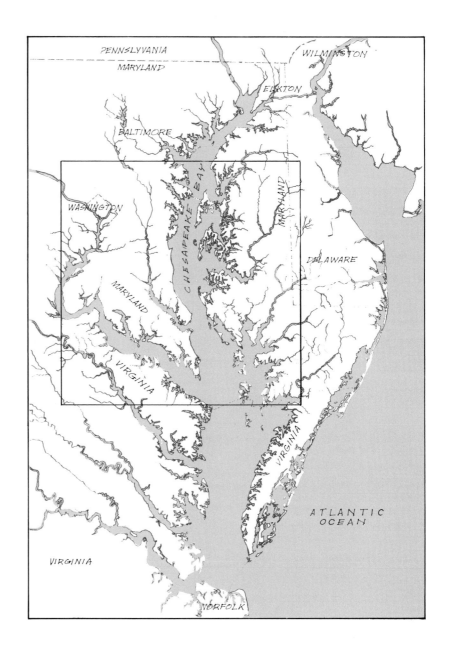

Table of Contents

List of Plates

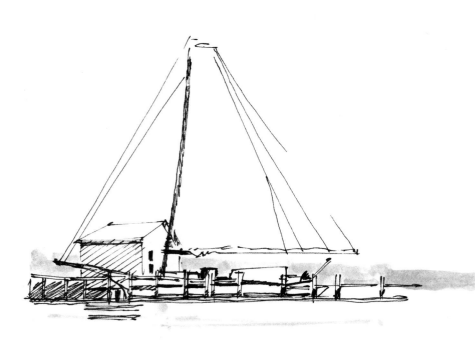

Preface

The bayside of Maryland's Eastern Shore is as special a place as can be found wherever land and water meet. Just ask the Shore native, whose family ties to the area are as tenacious as are the roots of the loblolly pine. Ask the newcomer, who willingly abandons his homeland to proudly announce an Eastern Shore address. Ask the tourist, who toils elsewhere fifty weeks a year in order to vacation for a short time on the Chesapeake shoreline. And browse through the books that have been published about the Eastern Shore. Their number grows larger each season and they reflect an enthusiasm that is unwavering.

There is no point in arguing against it: the Shore bayside is nearly unparalleled in its general appeal. This book certainly does not assume an opposing view, although it purposely does not draw an unabashed romantic portrait of the region. Both artist and narrator have felt the sting of the mosquito and nettle, the icy blast of February's wind, and the heavy cloak of August's humidity enough to know better than to depict the Shore as singularly flawless.

In a sense, *Bayside Impressions* may be considered a guidebook. Its itinerary begins with the clay banks of northern Kent County and follows the quaggy littoral to remote Smith Island, in the Bay off Crisfield in Somerset County. We hope that the unhurried observer will discover—or rediscover—the charms of the small villages and flat countryside described in the following pages. Additionally, this book may serve as a primer for those contemplating the use of paints and brushes. Few geographical regions offer the array of paintable sea- and landscapes as does Maryland's Shore. Remote as it may seem to be, the Eastern Shore is accessible and accommodating.

No single book can embody all that is the Eastern Shore. This one does not claim to do so. Instead, this book is a collaborative effort to describe in a kaleidoscope of impressions an Eastern Shore that is both remarkably pristine and threatened by the profanities of an increasing residential and tourist population. Much of the Eastern Shore remains picturesque and rustic. But its face is rapidly changing. This book attempts to capture its image as it is now.

At times the partnership between art and text appear to break. Quite simply, this is the result of two travelers, following the same path, casting glances in different directions. The effect, we believe, offers a unique sampling of Eastern Shore scenes, culture, and history.

J. D. I.
W. L. T.

Bayside Impressions

MARYLAND'S EASTERN SHORE AND THE CHESAPEAKE BAY

Kent County

From the steep, orange-colored banks of northern Kent County, the cannonading of artillery shells at Aberdeen Proving Ground just across the Chesapeake resounds in muffled, thunderous claps. It nearly loosens the sky over the tranquil Shore countryside. The firing of the shells at the practice range less than five miles away often is the loudest noise to be heard along Kent's shore. When the cannons are quiet, the dominant sound is the rush of wind through tree branches and, in summer, along rows of leafy cornstalks. Elsewhere, in the protected coves of Worton and Fairlee creeks, there is the dull tintinnabulation of halyards striking the aluminum masts of moored sailboats.

Decades ago steamboats puffed across the Bay from Baltimore harbor to the sandy resort towns of Tolchester and Betterton where sunbathing, swimming, amusement rides, and picnics awaited the city dwellers. Steamers such as the *Tolchester*, the *Louise*, and the popular *Emma Giles* pulled up to wide piers two hundred yards long and discharged passengers on a daily schedule.

Tolchester—the old Tolchester—is hardly recognizable now. Its bathhouses have been torn down, and the stately white hotel with the biggest screened-in porch on the Upper Shore was bulldozed into obscurity. For a while the booths housing pinball machines and other games of chance were allowed to stand on the bluff overlooking the beach. Vines grew undisturbed around the roller coaster tracks and up the sides of the little buildings until the entire park was cleared, a nearby marshy inlet was dredged, and a modern marina was built.

Betterton, to the north of Tolchester and snugly remote at the mouth of the Sassafras River, has been spared such a dramatic metamorphosis. It has become a hybrid of sorts, a cross between an unpressured resort town with a small but popular beach and a residential community of mansarded bungalows on the high ground nearby.

In winter, when February ice on the Sassafras breaks with the movement of the tides and is shoved onto the beach in uneven, jagged layers, and the small number of resort businesses are boarded up, the town is cloaked in a somber desuetude. As spring approaches, hammers and paint brushes are applied to building and pier; there is a spirited attempt to spruce up the beach area. But tourists do not come to Betterton as they once did. Even the motorcycle clubs that roared into town from Wilmington and Philadelphia for an evening of booze and juke box come less often.

The heyday of steamboat excursions is gone (the *Port Welcome*, in the late seventies under diesel power, was the last passenger boat to visit Betterton) and a dwindling group of businessmen is the only segment of the town's population that misses that profitable era. Most residents like Betterton just the way it is—cleaner and quieter than it has been in years.

South of Betterton and Tolchester, ensconced on the lower lip of a natural harbor, is the rugged little town of Rock Hall. For many years Rock Hall had the reputation of being a tough place, a town where an outsider should watch his step, where it was not healthy to get into anybody's bad books.

Over the past two decades retirees from Baltimore and from the southside of Philadelphia have moved to the outskirts of Rock Hall, somewhat diluting the boisterous air of the town. But still the reputation clings.

Rock Hallers, it is said in unkind generalizations, are clannish, roguish, and, at times, uncouth; they drink too much, talk too loud, and drive too fast. They have a penchant for fighting with very little provocation, and they usually win their fights because they have no fear of being bloodied.

Even the town itself—the waterfront with its sagging docks and the main street with its bars—has been maligned. Rock Hall, some claimed, smelled bad. Outside the

BLUE SIGN

CA

RED LETTERS

TREES

ROCK HALL

JAMES DRAKE IAMS

packing houses was a mountain of shucked oyster shells. This mass of wet and muddy refuse was not a problem as long as the weather remained cold. But when the July and August sun drifted overhead, the shells nearly baked, and a foul odor drifted through the town where it commingled with the mildly repugnant vapors rising from the steam vats in the tomato cannery.

The brickbats tossed at Rock Hall's character come generally from the county's hinterland and particularly from the more genteel, less weather-beaten seat of local government—Chestertown. Proudly displaying its colonial-era vestiges, Chestertown is the Upper Shore's answer to the quintessential tour book example of wealth, conservativism, grace, charm, and hauteur. Along the Chester River waterfront red-bricked manors, preserved with great care, face the wide, unhurried river. The center of town is an arrangement of scenes suitable for postcards. There is the iron fountain in the park, the thick-trunked trees and the heavy cannon, the courthouse, the renovated inn with its neatly hand-painted sign, the brick sidewalks, and the main street leading down to the river where a dozen or so mallards feed and preen throughout the year. At the edge of town, on a slight rise known locally as "the hill," Washington College sits, more than two hundred years old and the only academic institution in the country to which the first president sanctioned in writing the use of his name. Novelist James Cain, who studied and taught at the college at the turn of the century during his father's term as president, is said to have developed a style for tough dialogue by listening to the banterings of laborers laying the bricks for the sidewalk that runs by the campus.

Rock Hall, on the other hand, is rough around the edges. Its colonial mansions are few. Its sidewalks are uneven paths of concrete, and its main street might not look so plain if there were more trees—leafy trees—growing there.

But Rock Hall is a waterman's town where soiled hands and hard luck are essential to its demeanor. Those who live there choose to do so without resenting their town's

Hubbard's Dock, Rock Hall

CHESAPEAKE
ICE · BAIT · TACKLE

MARYANN

JAMES DRAKE IAMS A.W.S. ©83

lack of refinement. Any antagonism between them and their Chestertown cousins is merely healthy tension. (Similar relationships are shared by other towns along the Shore: Queenstown and Centreville, Tilghman and Easton, Crisfield and Princess Anne. It is nothing new, and it is sure to last a while.)

At any rate, Rock Hall no longer offends the nose. The oyster shell pile is gone; the shells were hauled away to fill holes in dirt farm lanes or were carried by boat and dumped into the Bay to form seedbeds for more oysters. The tomato cannery is quiet and vapor-free. Weeds grow where the workers parked their cars and pickups. Rock Hall is less noisy as well, except occasionally in summer when sailors and motorists stop by to picnic at Ingleside Beach and Bogel's Wharf.

The decline in the commercial seafood industry has affected every bayside town. Poor catches of oysters, crabs, and rock (striped bass) in the upper portions of the Bay have forced Rock Hall's watermen to sail south to Kent Narrows, Tilghman Island, and even to Crisfield. Any farther down the Bay and the workboats would be in Virginia waters.

Rock Hall's harbor was filled with workboats in better days. The Bay's fleet of skipjacks, now few in number and rarely seen above the twin Bay bridges, once anchored at Rock Hall. Some other, less peripatetic watermen who lived in town built tiny wooden sheds which were mounted onto skids. When the crab or oyster season opened, the mobile shanties were dragged down to the water's edge and filled with the gear needed to harvest catches. When the season closed, the sheds were shoved back into town and left beside the owner's house. Some of these odd but functional structures remain in Rock Hall, but they are never taken to the water any more.

A century ago Rock Hall businessmen were enthusiastic about promoting the virtues of their bustling bayside village. The seafood harvests were bringing money to the town, and community leaders were calling for expansion and diversification of commerce.

EMPTY
BASKETS
IN SHADOW

VIOLET
SHIRT

GRAY
BLUE
PANTS

JAMES DRAKE IAMS

BREAK TIME

Since Rock Hall had been the Eastern Shore terminus of the ferry system as early as the eighteenth century and passenger boats continued to drop off travelers, it was suggested that something be done to keep the wayfarers in Rock Hall.

At the time there was substantial concern among city dwellers of Baltimore and Washington, D. C., that a malarial epidemic was imminent. Rock Hall, declared the town physician, was virtually free of "bad air" (the connection between malaria and mosquitoes had not yet been solidly established). The Shore's pine forests impregnated the atmosphere with ozone, believed to be a natural antiseptic against malaria. Rock Hall, bounded inland with pine, it seemed was the perfect location for a grand health resort.

The local doctor enlisted the aid of the state physician, and a pamphlet was published extolling the wondrous effects a prolonged stay in Rock Hall could have on a cough-wracked body. It began with an enticing caveat:

> Persons visiting the Eastern Shore who are unaccustomed to breathing the air are likely to experience at first excelerated [sic] circulation, palpitations, nuralgic [sic] pains (where there is excessive nervous irritability), insomnia, etc.; but by degrees— after twenty-four or forty-eight hours—they become, as it were, acclimated, and all perturbations and pains disappear.

The omnipresent ozone, said the good doctor, was the cause and cure of all this. He continued:

> . . . in twenty years I never saw a case of consumption, nor ever a case of asthma or hay fever, spring or autumn, and have known seven cases of both entirely relieved within twenty-four hours after reaching here.

It was best to visit Rock Hall in the fall, he advised, to get accustomed to breathing the air, and in the meantime the town's popular Chesapeake House restaurant (which had

Oyster Tonger, Fishing Creek, Hooper Island

JAMES DRAKE IAMS A.W.S. ©83

coincidentally taken out a half-page advertisement in the pamphlet) was sure to be open for business "with table supplied with fish, oysters, crabs and game in season."

If it was true then, it remains so now. Rock Hall is no less a sanatorium than it ever has been, except that much of its pine forests have been cleared, possibly reducing the ozone level somewhat.

Rock Hall is both bay- and creek-oriented. To the southeast creeks flowing into the Chester River curl inland toward town. If Grays Inn Creek, for example, was any closer to town, it would take little effort to cut a canal joining the harbor to the creek, putting much of Rock Hall on a new island.

Modest houses, strung like dissimilar beads on a wire, line the creek banks wherever the ground passed the local percolation tests. Some of the structures are spanking new with expensive bulkheading to prevent the water from eroding the tiny lots. Other, older homes have lost their luster and are in need of paint. Where there is no bulkheading, the water touches a slip of sandy soil dense with vegetation; the shoreline takes on a wavering contour, rising several feet with the erosion-control devices and dipping where there is none.

Nearly every house has a dock, and every dock one or two small boats. As the creeks narrow, the water becomes shallow so that at low tide the boats tied there list to one side.

Workboats rigged for clamming year-round and for crabbing in spring and summer are tied up in the deeper waters of Grays Inn Creek off the public landing at Herrington. There, at a family-operated marina, are enough slips for a dozen workboats. But sailboats and cabin cruisers belonging to weekend sailors from Delaware and Pennsylvania are increasingly more common than workboats in the creek.

Much of the east side of Grays Inn Creek gives way to marshland. Patches of cattails and stretches abundant with yellow reeds protrude from the shallows. The standard population of the marsh coexists in summer with the boaters chattering and banging about on the opposite shoreline. Songbirds, shy white swan, ducks, muskrats, and an occasional deer go about their seasonal routines with benign scornfulness. Spits of muddy sand jutting out into the creek are patrolled by the solitary blue heron. A boat rounding a bend will cause the heron to spread its tremendous wings, retract its long legs, and kink its neck as it flies into a circling pattern overhead until the disturbance has passed. With all its apparent ungainliness, the heron can settle onto a tree limb with surprising grace. In addition to being one of the most timid birds on the Shore, the heron is absolutely mute except during the short mating season when it engages in a one-to-one chase at great speeds through the air, emitting its gravelly ululation. It is most cacophonous, sounding something like the honk of a Canada goose played in reverse at a slow speed. Among its own kind, however, the outcry is a lovesong.

Here and there along the shoreline and back into tidal ponds abandoned duck and goose blinds give the marshes a remotely crenellated look. The wooden structures have been turned gray by the weather. Their weight causes the stilts upon which they are affixed to sink unevenly into the mud. Wind has unfastened some of the plywood walls, and the sections lie flat upon the marsh grass much as they must have when being first assembled.

Deserted blinds, twisted piers, and dung-capped channel markers are favorite nesting sites for the osprey or fish hawk. The carnivorous bird weaves branches thick as a broom handle into well-ventilated, remarkably sturdy nests. Summer gales that tear limbs from trees and break boats from their moorings barely disturb these roosts.

Somewhere—the precise location is a matter of lively speculation in history-conscious Kent County—three hundred years ago on the northern shores of Grays Inn Creek the village of New Yarmouth was bustling with river traffic and with matters of importance to a new seat of county government. New Yarmouth had been laid out on paper first. Narrow streets made it a grid pattern with lots of equal size for modest houses and little gardens. Some warehouses had been built near the water to protect the valuable tobacco and other commodities necessary for a mercantile community. A church with a stone foundation was erected near the town center; its spire was the highest point in the neat but otherwise undistinguished village.

Materially wealthy but politically dissatisfied families had moved to the area from Kent Island several miles to the south so that they could establish a new center of government, a government designed more according to their wishes. Political fortunes changed hands within several years after New Yarmouth had been founded and the Grays Inn Creek site was determined unsuitable by others more influential in the colonial government. Chestertown, farther up the Chester River and deep within the rich farm country, became the county seat. New Yarmouth was abandoned by nearly all who lived there. Some buildings were dismantled and moved. The local shipwrights packed their tools and relocated elsewhere where their trade was in demand.

New Yarmouth existed so temporarily that written records of what happened there exist today in but a few pages of manuscript and in a number of vague references. No one is sure where the town was located, although there are those amateur historians who claim to have deduced from the scanty records available that New Yarmouth was at this spot or at that spot. A popular belief is that the town was built on the tip of Grays Inn Point, now a snub of farmland conspicuous more than anything else for the method of erosion control used on its starboard shoreline. A decade or two ago old automobiles, trucks, and pieces of farm equipment were pushed over the edge of a cornfield where they dropped fifteen or so feet to the clay beach below. They remain there rusty and

Break Time, Tilghman Island

ineffectual, their use as a kind of Detroit riprap hardly worth the sweat it took to shove them down the bank.

Not far away, out in the water a few hundred yards to the south, there may be some relics of old New Yarmouth. More than once sailors rounding the point in the shallow waters at low tide have felt their hulls thumping against some very hard objects. Since the river bottom usually is very soft and muddy at the mouth to Grays Inn Creek, it quite naturally was wondered what was the source of the bumps. Somebody claimed to have investigated and discovered a number of large stones arranged in a foundationlike pattern in the mud. These stones, certainly not indigenous to the area, are believed to be what remains of the New Yarmouth church.

Eastern Neck, stretching due south for four miles from Huntingfield Point directly below Rock Hall Harbor to Wilson Point, offers one of the most unobstructed views of the upper Chesapeake. From the slightly concave bayside shoreline one can see the smog over Baltimore on the western shore down to the Bay bridges linking Sandy Point and Kent Island. Eastern Neck is barely a mile at its widest stretch. Its eastern face is cut with broad coves and marshes and two creeks, the navigable Grays Inn and the too shallow Church. State Route 445, said to be the oldest highway in the country still in use, runs from Rock Hall to Eastern Neck, over the water and onto the island. In late fall and throughout winter the shorn cornfields are filled with thousands of Canada geese. As they become accustomed to the passing of traffic on the road, they feed and preen unbothered just yards from the shoulders.

Beneath the Eastern Neck Island bridge, an old wooden structure, the tidal waters are shallow and slow moving. The mud flats are patrolled by herons and muskrats. In summer the waters are shedding grounds for crabs, who skirt about in their peculiar sideways flights from one clump of bay grass to another. The flats have been a favorite spot for soft-crabbing by local boys and girls. Aluminum rowboats may

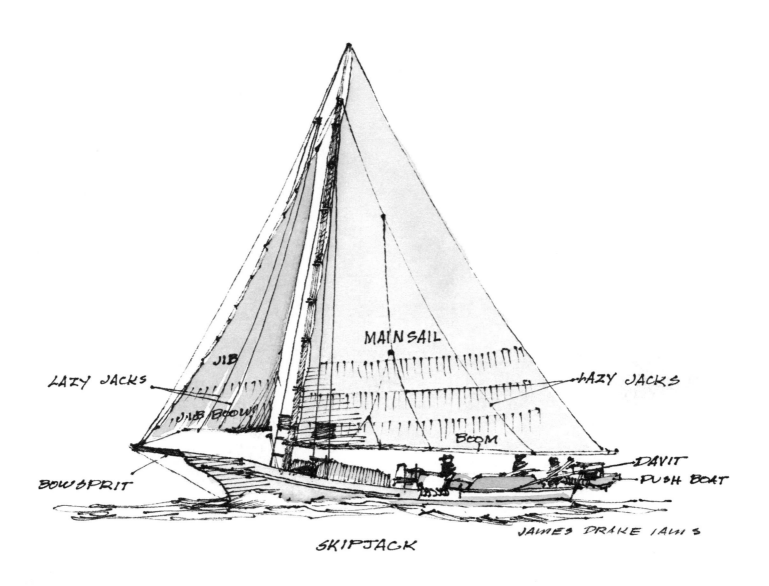

JIB

LAZY JACKS

JIB BOOM

MAINSAIL

LAZY JACKS

BOOM

DAVIT

PUSH BOAT

BOWSPRIT

JAMES DRAKE IAMS

SKIPJACK

be rented nearby, and with a dipnet and a keen eye the fragile but feisty soft crabs can be caught with little trouble.

The bridge, too, is a popular spot for fishing and crabbing. But local highway officials, mindful that pedestrians and motor vehicles should not share the same swath of blacktop, have tried to keep people off the bridge. A sign was posted on the Eastern

Neck side warning all that there would be "No Fishing No Swimming No Grabbing." (The humorous typographical error was replaced soon after with a more authoritative caveat against using the bridge for recreation.)

Eastern Neck Island is managed as a wildlife refuge under the United States Fish and Wildlife Service. There are several buildings, privately owned, on the island, and some of the land is planted with corn and soybean. Nature trails cut through the thick brush to the beaches and marshes where picnic tables are set up. But for the most part the island is a quiet area with little activity except for the routines of animal life.

Indians inhabited the woods on Eastern Neck Island. They hunted waterfowl and deer and caught crabs and oysters. They buried their dead on the island's bayside. Not long ago the brittle white bones of a skeleton were half exposed in a shallow grave cut open by the sloshing Bay. Eastern Neck Island, too, is eroding.

By late May the cream-colored flowers of the honeysuckle vine are blossoming against a background of green and brown. Migratory birds have been gone for several months. But for the occasional pair of mallards in a water-filled ditch and black ducks in the marsh, it is the songbird that is most plentiful. No other bird so epitomizes the Shore in warm weather as the epauletted red-winged blackbird perched on the stem of a tall, green reed at water's edge.

Spring and early summer rains keep tidal levels at their highest. The ground is saturated with water and during a day of unobstructed sunlight many sorts of vegetation grow thick and fast. Later, when cornfields are lined with young shoots, farmers will say they can hear the corn growing. Ticks cling to every blade of grass. Mosquitoes rise hungrily from the ditches and marshes. In the water minnows are plump and numerous. They churn the surface as they feed and are fed upon by larger fish. Water snakes—their rusty-colored scales arranged in ferocious patterns—sun themselves on the trunks of fallen trees and upon planks washed onto the marsh grass. Rabbits dash in crisscrosses over open fields while hawks float overhead.

Eel pots are set out in the Chester River and checked daily by watermen who hope to accumulate several hundred pounds worth to soak in plastic barrels filled with brine. The eels will be cut into sections and tied onto trotlines as bait when the blue crab arrives in a few weeks.

The mouth of the Chester River turns upward and wide into the Chesapeake like the bowl of a calabash pipe. Eastern Neck Island sits in the inner curve of the stem. On weekends sailboats, their white sails intermittently billowed, puff around in the Bay until evening leaves the air breezeless and the water glassy. Then, under power of their inboard motors, the boats slip up the river and into quiet coves protected by sandy spits of land. Anchors are dropped and charcoal grills, hung at the stern over the water, are fueled. Some sailors prefer to spend the night in solitude. The gregarious lash their gunwales together to form long rafts of up to a dozen boats; the partying can last until daybreak.

The days get steamier. By July the lament "it's-not-the-heat-it's-the-humidity" is common. But already, in late May, thunderstorms briefly tear apart the dank cloak that hangs over land and water. Before the storm strikes, the air becomes still and scented with an acidlike aroma. Birds become quiet, and the sky darkens as gray-black clouds roll above like enormous, noisy logs. For a minute or two the wind picks up, and then the clouds pour out such a deluge that dust becomes mud instantly and creeks turn to a roiling stew of splashes, twigs, and sediment. On land the storm is almost welcome. It cools the air until the sun reappears to start the cycle anew. On water the swiftness of the Chesapeake squall is well known. Boats unable to reach a safe harbor or to anchor in the prescribed fashion are pitched about with abandon. Sodden sails are ripped by the wind and anything or anybody topside risks being thrown overboard. Watermen who have sailed the Bay for decades know that avoiding the squall is the surest way to survive it.

Queen Anne's County

As a subject of contempt, the Chesapeake Bay bridges suffer a notoriety in Queen Anne's County accorded elsewhere on the Shore only to the mosquito. Animosity toward the twin structures joining the two sides of the Bay is felt not only by many native Shoremen who believe life here has been irreversibly altered for the worse because of the bridges, but also by those who have lived in the region a short time. Newcomers to the Shore—called foreigners by the natives—often embrace the unhurried rural life with such enthusiasm that they become jingoistic. Having secured their place in "the land of pleasant living," they now hope for some way of stopping others from moving into the same area. (In many instances, this sentiment is quite justified. Following the 1952 opening of the first bridge, housing development in Queen Anne's County, specifically on the waterfronts of Kent Island, raced ahead of planning and zoning ordinances. Homes were built upon soil that would not pass modern percolation standards. Community sewer and water systems remain outdated and insufficient to meet increasing demands.)

The tension between Shore natives and foreigners is exaggerated at times. Certainly on Kent Island, the eastern terminus of the bridges, the at-odds relationship is more history than a part of everyday life. The reason is simple: There are more foreigners living on the island today than native Shoremen. And those who have lived or summered on the island for more than two or three decades sometimes assume a proprietary air, as though twenty or thirty years of living in one area carried with it the social sinecure of a family whose roots can be traced to several generations. And the real old-timers are those who moved to Kent Island before the bridges were built; they recall the days of the ferry boats, which stopped sailing on this part of the Bay in the fifties.

Up in the county, however, in the middle of farm country where the towns with no more than one or two traffic lights actually have changed little since the bridge opened, the distinction between who is native and who is interloper remains very clear. Consider this anecdote: Years and years ago a young married couple from the western shore bought a small piece of land, had a home built, moved in, and raised a family. The husband, one day after his retirement from his job, was raking leaves in his backyard. His neighbor, who lived in the house his great granddaddy had built, was in his yard raking leaves. The two got to talking and the first fellow said to his neighbor, "Let me ask you a question that's been on my mind for some time. Now, I know my wife and I aren't Eastern Shore natives. But we came here when we were very young and had children and they grew up right here. My question is, wouldn't you consider them to be Eastern Shore natives?" His neighbor stood in silence for a moment, and replied, "Well now, if a cat jumps in an oven and has a litter, you don't call the kittens biscuits, do ya?"

Another story of a similar vein retold within the county is concerned with the newspaper obituary headline of a woman who died in her nineties near the county seat of Centreville. The woman had lived all but the first two months of her life in Queen Anne's County, having been carried across the Bay as an infant by her parents from her native Baltimore. The obituary notice gave the normal attention to the particulars of her life, that she had attended the local schools, was married to a native son, had reared their children here, and had served in numerous community organizations with distinction. She was popular and respected as a kind matron. It was without derision and quite proper when, scanning the obituary text for material, a headline writer set in bold copy "Baltimore Woman Dies At Age 92."

Those natives throughout the Shore who occasionally rue that muggy, late-July morning in 1952 when the first bridge was opened to public traffic do so with mixed feelings. The subsequent, almost immediate influx of foreigners altered the landscape as well as the way of life on the Shore. A building trade blossomed, and the old but low-key tourism industry took tremendous strides in commercializing sections along the highways.

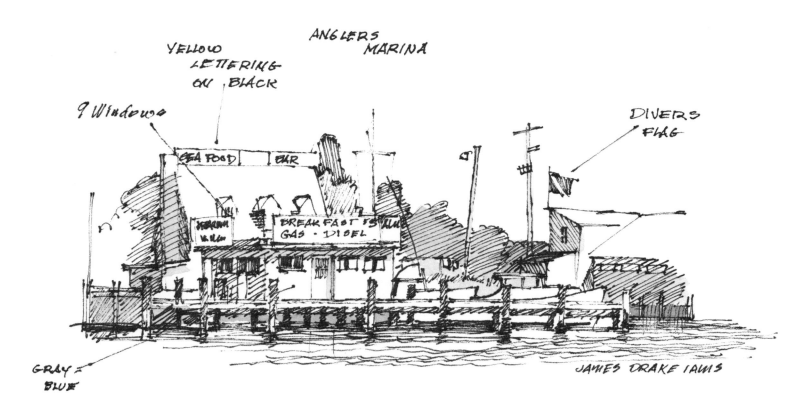

It would have happened wherever the Bay bridge touched the Shore—the transformation of a drowsy, bucolic setting to a blend of housing development, marina, and dual highway, the latter embellished without much concern for aesthetics with fast food, fast gas, and slow traffic. That Kent Island was selected to receive the cross-Bay traffic fits a logic that is hard to dispute. The Sandy Point-Kent Island connection is convenient for western shore travelers and the two points make up one of the shortest distances between the shores. Even the entrepreneurial facet of Kent Island has a historical precedent. Three years before Lord Baltimore established his settlement at St. Mary's in what is now Southern Maryland, the colonial scofflaw William Claiborne landed at Winston, changed its name to Kent Island, and initiated a trading post—a commercial business—that became the most troublesome burr under Lord Baltimore's saddle for years.

Also on Kent Island, specifically at its southernmost point, occurred one of the first recorded crimes on the Shore involving European colonists. This tale of murder is as cloudy as Bay water, however. Someone—an Indian, a French pirate, or one of Lord Baltimore's men—was hanged within the vicinity known now as Bloody Point.

Bloody Point. Love Point. Matapeake. Sharktown. Crab Alley. The island's place-names conjure visions of an era less hurried, more rooted in survival, to the days of Indians, traders, vessels under sail, and watermen in oilskins. The development of Kent Island was gradual. Trails cut by Indians were trod by colonists, then cut wider and eventually covered with oyster shells. The main on-island route running north to south was not paved until early in this century, and then, it is said, those who lived nearby thought it an unnecessary luxury, even though it ended the annoying oyster-shell dust kicked up and blown everywhere whenever it was traveled. Before the tar-and-chip had cooled, it also is said, islanders living by the lower end of Route 8 gathered on the road at dusk and had one of the finest crap games ever; the dice rolled well on the even surface.

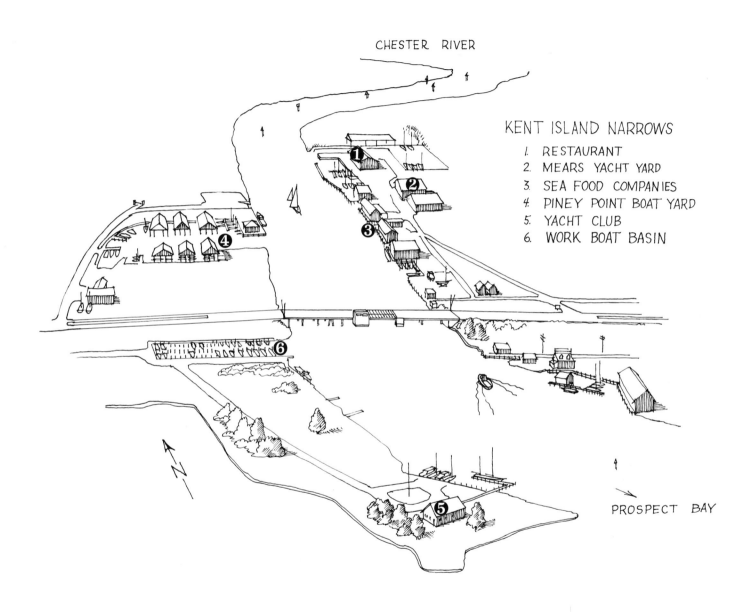

CHESTER RIVER

KENT ISLAND NARROWS

1. RESTAURANT
2. MEARS YACHT YARD
3. SEA FOOD COMPANIES
4. PINEY POINT BOAT YARD
5. YACHT CLUB
6. WORK BOAT BASIN

PROSPECT BAY

Subdivisions filled with prefabricated houses now take up more land on the island than do farms. Place-names are adopted with expediency. Streets are bestowed with names of trees and states; developments are named after plants, coves, and tidewater plantations. Restaurants use the words fisherman or angler in their names. There is a race, lost by all involved, to build something new and make it sound like something old.

The population shift in Queen Anne's County since the opening of the bridges has been the cause for some alarm by the county's traditionally strong Democrats. For decades there was little representation in local politics from the island. The county's northeastern flat lands, soil-rich and seasonally thick with corn and soybeans, was and remains the source of political power. With all its waterfront and watermen, the region has been ruled by up-county farmers and landowners. The county seat was relocated in Centreville because, it was justifiably argued, the town was situated near the center of Queen Anne's. It was accessible to the agrarian population and could carry on commerce via the water through its landing on the Corsica River.

Queenstown, perched closer to the Bay on the eastern shores of the Chester River, was the original site of county government. Now it is epicentral to the population. To the west, from Grasonville to Chester and Stevensville on Kent Island, the population is fairly dense. To the east, from Centreville to Sudlersville, housing developments are rare and families are relatively sparse. (In some respects Queenstown never forgave Centreville for "taking away" its courthouse and its pride as a political base. Friction between the two towns is taken out on the softball diamonds and through general conversations in which Queenstown is pictured as podunk and Centreville as snobbish. Queenstown can be satisfied, in a sense, that while its courthouse was "moved," it still has the small but visible dray of white squirrels who apparently took happily to the large, nut-bearing trees in the area after they were set free there by a sea captain who captured them in a now-forgotten land.)

Angler's Marina, Kent Narrows

The county's newest residents—those on Kent Island and the nearby areas—are beginning to flex political muscles. Coming to Queen Anne's with the expectation that community services constitute a quid pro quo for paying taxes, they are demanding that they receive attention from the Centreville politicians. Some are even running for public office. Not long ago one of the island newcomers challenged the status quo political system in the county by making a bid for office as a Republican and showing up at rallies dressed in a three-piece suit, two maneuvers traditionally frowned upon in the region.

Six days a week the glare of pickup truck headlights and the throaty roar of diesel inboards awaken a small section of manmade shoreline at the Kent Narrows. For more than a century, gathering at the Narrows, watermen have gotten up and readied their workboats long before the sun's slow upward climb. The water there is swift and deep, but the location on the eastern lip of the island a few hundred yards from the mainland is safe and convenient. Crabs and clams are plentiful just north in the Chester River; crabs, clams, and oysters are caught just south in the expanse of shallow Eastern Bay.

In recent years the county has carved out the shoreline and dredged the bottom to create a rectangular basin for workboats belonging to local watermen. Several scores of white, wooden boats outfitted with hydraulic rigs and with shaft tongs laid fore-to-aft are tied up in the slips.

Across the way, on the opposite shore, are concrete-block packing houses where the day's catches are sold and there are fuel pumps and several boat yards. Nearly all the waterman's needs are met at the Narrows, excepting, of course, someone else to do his hard day's work for him.

The concrete-and-steel drawbridge that crosses the Narrows is neither picturesque nor unattractive. Its progenitors were made of wood and were narrow with a single lane

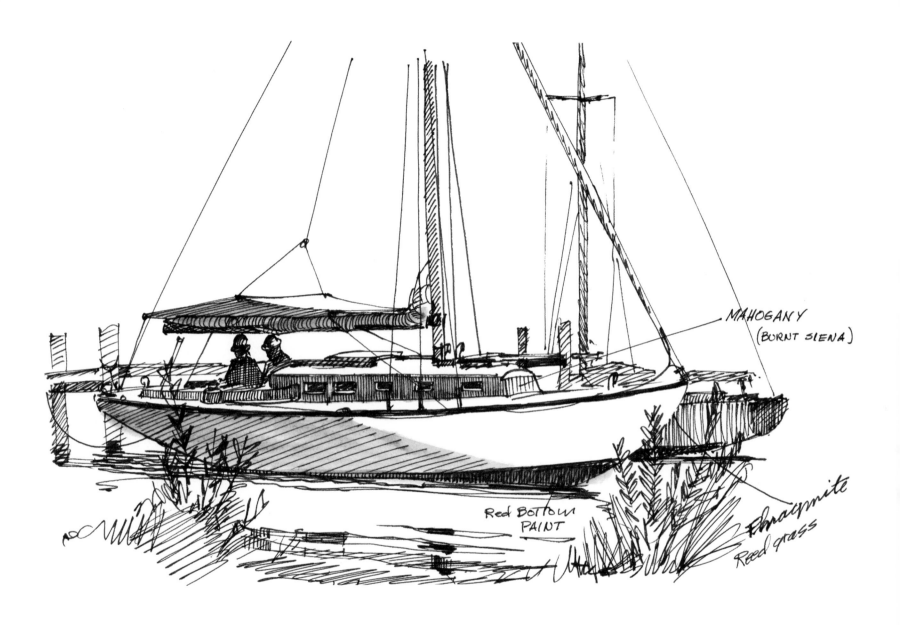

MAHOGANY
(BURNT SIENA)

Red Bottom
PAINT

Phragmite
Reed grass

rising a few feet above the water. It was rebuilt with four lanes soaring nearly twenty feet over the estuary. Passage by automobile over and by boat under takes but a few seconds, and in many cases it is the least conspicuous bridge on the Shore's main thoroughfare.

But no body of water, no length of roadway on the entire Shore has been the source of so much debate and frustration. By late May, when the honeysuckle flowers on land and the puffball clouds overhead brighten the drab brown residue of winter, the western shore seems to conspire to send everything with tires and horns east, rumbling across Kent Island toward the Atlantic beaches. Cars, motorcycles, and trucks towing boats and campers pour onto the Shore by land; by water come fleets of sail and power boats. All appear to want to navigate Kent Narrows, either on or below the bridge, at the same time.

There would be no problem except that the Narrows bridge has a draw span that must be raised periodically to let pleasure boaters pass (the clearance between the water and the bridge is insufficient for most of the Bay sailboats, although workboats move back and forth under the structure with ease).

On any given summer weekend the number of vehicles to cross the Narrows averages at two thousand per hour, a figure that rivals traffic in downtown Manhattan. When the drawspan was raised hourly to let sailboats navigate through the Narrows, the backup of road traffic stretched out ten or more miles from the bridge. Bridge openings for boats have been rescheduled in favor of motor vehicles, yet the unmoving, unbroken successions of cars and trucks continue. When the draw span goes up and highway traffic comes to a stop, drivers and passengers empty onto the roadway. For fifteen or twenty minutes, or at times much longer, Routes 301/50 on the western end of the county become the longest parking lot in the state.

Tempers can spill onto the roadway, too. Police report occasional fights following otherwise minor fender-bender collisions. Soft drinks, beers, and even shaving cream

Shipping Creek, Kent Island

have been poured and sprayed onto cars. Drivers have been seen relieving themselves at the shoulder of the road (said one officer who witnessed such an incident, "I guess it's somewhat understandable. He didn't want to lose his place in line").

When the span is lowered and the traffic grinds slowly on its way, sailboats approaching the Narrows must drop anchor and wait for the next opening, or take the five-hour sail around the island. Water racing through the Narrows during tidal changes is swift (a bridge tender fell into the drink; in less than a minute he was swept two hundred yards toward Eastern Bay). Sailors must leave plenty of space between themselves and other boats or the channel will knock them together like some discordant water chime.

While all this is going on, those who live above and below the highway find it virtually impossible to cross over to the other side. Going out for a loaf of bread can be a tribulation.

There is much more to the Queen Anne's wetlands than the busy jumble of marinas, restaurants, traffic jams, and condominiums that greet the motorist passing through via the Routes 301/50 corridor. The sailor sees this, and so does the casual driver willing to follow secondary roads.

Great portions of shoreline exist as they must have in the days of John Smith and William Claiborne. On the Queen Anne's side of the Chester River, as far up as the mouth of the Corsica where the Russians are ensconced in the magnificent red-brick manor house of the late and well-known American capitalist John J. Raskob, sandy beaches reveal themselves at low tide before thick, dark woods of pine and holly. Tiny creeks and guts bend around bright spits of yellow sand and into marshy, tidal ponds where herons stalk for minnows and pairs of white swans paddle along the distant shore.

At morning and then at dusk deer leave the cool shadows of the wooded areas and walk along the beaches. Ectoskeletons with the pointed harmless dagger-tails of the horseshoe crab lie half-buried in the sand. Trotline and eel pot floats are caught in the tall grass or jammed between the twisted exposed roots of upturned trees.

Saltwater ponds are thick with catfish. In midsummer rays, or skates as they are known in local parlance, glide up creeks and feed upon the leaf-covered bottom mud or thrash the water with their wings.

South of Kent Narrows are Prospect Bay and Crab Alley Bay, opening into Eastern Bay. Inland are a number of creeks and points, and the Wye River, perhaps the most serpentine of all the Shore's rivers.

It was to this area that a young architect from New York City was called to design a manor house for a New York advertising executive. Although he was considered one of the best among the new breed of architects, Joel Barber's name thrives more with the cognoscenti of the decoy carving world. Barber lived in Centreville for a year while he oversaw the building of his design down by Prospect Bay. In his free time he motored about the county in his Ford, exploring the least traveled roads and inquiring of the local denizens the methods for building log canoes or gunning the black duck.

Barber wrote one of the first texts on decoys and their carvers; he is credited with establishing the wooden decoy as an American folk art. Barber also wrote poetry during his stay in Queen Anne's County and saw much of it published in the Centreville weekly. One of them reads as follows:

> Last spring I bought an old house,
> An old house on the Eastern Shore,
> A brick house by a quiet creek
> That flows along always, quietly,
> Then joins the Chester River.
>
> I fixed it up, this old house,
> Leveled floors, repaired the stair,
> Glazed broken panes, and afterwards
> Pointed up the chimneys and finally
> Hung curtains of lace at windows.
>
> It's winter now and cold winds
> Cry in the eaves of my old house.
> But fires burn in the old place
> And wood-smoke drifts again
> Along the creek and over the river.

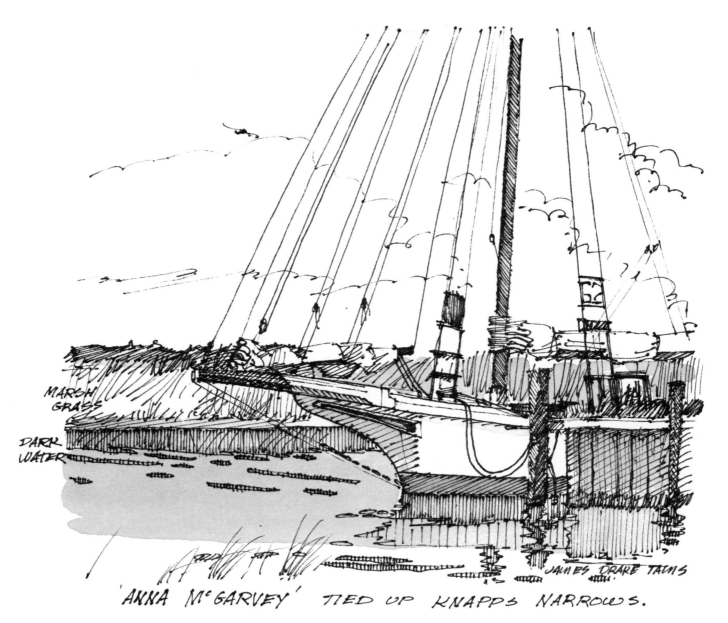

MARSH
GRASS

DARK
WATER

JAMES DRAKE TAWS

'ANNA MºGARVEY' TIED UP KNAPPS NARROWS.

And that old creek, opalescent in old glass,
Looks silver on a winter afternoon,
And over a fire of white oak,
Breast down in a shining range,
Prime canvasback are roasting now.

And here I live on a glamorous shore
In a homely sort of splendor.
Life steals by on crimson carpets
And I—for want of better names—
Call it—Living *à la Maryland*.

ORANGE FORD
TRUCK

Talbot County

If the Shore's bayside counties are pearls on a string, Talbot residents fancy their county the most cultured. Talbot Countians are at once down-to-earth and aristocratic, progressive and venerable. From the web-footed watermen of Tilghman Island to the well-heeled patricians of Oxford and St. Michaels, they manage a discreet compromise between tradition and progress, an ensemble that works nowhere better on the Shore.

Talbot is as much water as it is land; the water is sailable, making the land extremely saleable, and property values from the Wye River to the Choptank are among the highest in rural Maryland. Talbot County, the locals say, is one of two counties in the nation with the highest number of resident millionaires (nobody seems to remember the name of the other county). It's a pardonable exaggeration to say that there are as many Mercedes as pickup trucks on the county's backroads.

Swaddled in the mid-Shore safely away from the commercial hubbub of Queen Anne's Kent Island to the north and the marshy nether land of Dorchester County to the south, Talbot's many fingers of land curl into the Bay to form dozens of coves, bights, and bends. It is as natural a hideaway for today's overstressed executives as it was in centuries past for pirates.

Easton, hard by Route 50 and its sleeve of fast-food restaurants, is the county's business and cultural center. Its downtown section is a living museum of restored post-colonial houses, tree-lined avenues marked with wrought iron street signs, a courtyard with a statue of a Confederate soldier, an exclusive yacht club, movie theatres, a daily newspaper, one of the best hospitals on the Shore, and tastefully decorated lounges patronized by Oxford-shirted, penny-loafered regulars. On the outskirts Easton offers a blend of shopping center, light industry, and farmland.

Tilghman Island hangs out into the Bay like the claw of some angry rooster ready to strike. The tip of the talon is Black Walnut Point; for a number of years local residents have been waiting for it to be shed. Erosion is so great on the bayside that the Army Corps of Engineers has predicted that unless measures are taken to stop it, the point may become Black Walnut Island by the mid-1990s. On very blustery days, cars driven along the only blacktop road there, parallelling the shoreline, are covered with salt spray. The Corps has suggested that a revetment of stones weighing more than two tons each be laid along a 375-foot piece of the shore to ensure that the seventy-four acres of land, four houses, and a naval research station remain part of the main island.

The absence of spring rains and winds—a rarity—is relished by the islanders, particularly by the young little leaguers who find it nearly impossible to play ball behind the island's elementary school when the lot is soggy. Throughout winter and spring the western side of the island is battered by wave action. The beaches are strewn with fallen timber.

When a national advertising firm decided to film a beer commercial depicting rugged watermen armed with heavy oilskins against a cold and challenging sea, working feverishly until they could return to port and enjoy their favorite brew, they chose Tilghman Island and a number of its skipjacks as principal characters.

Several of the Bay's skipjacks, representing the depleted fleet of wooden vessels that go after oysters under sail, are owned by Tilghman Islanders. When oyster season

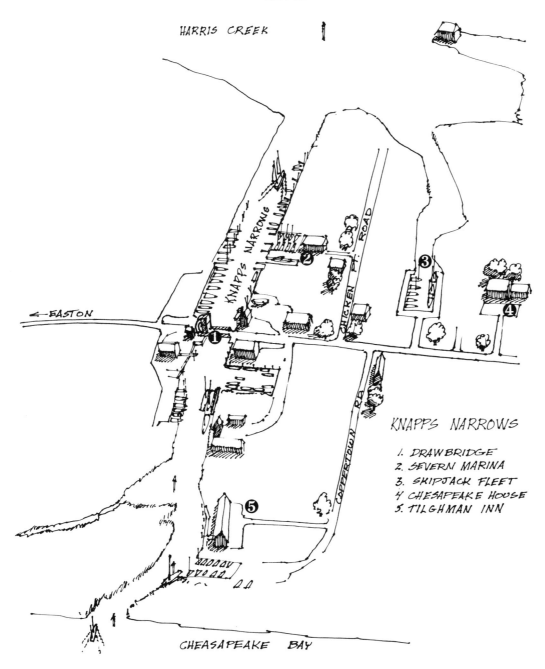

CHOPTANK RIVER

HARRIS CREEK

KNAPPS NARROWS

KNAPPS NARROWS

←EASTON

CHICKEN PT. ROAD

COPPERTOWN RD.

KNAPPS NARROWS

1. DRAWBRIDGE
2. SEVERN MARINA
3. SKIPJACK FLEET
4. CHESAPEAKE HOUSE
5. TILGHMAN INN

CHEASAPEAKE BAY

begins, the skipjack captains are instant media celebrities, responding to reporters' inquiries about the fortunes of the bivalve crop with typically feigned indifference.

"How's the season look to you, Cap'n," a brief interview will begin, punctuated throughout with long pauses while the skipper finds some chore to do.

"Well, I figger it'll be purty good and then it'll be bad before it gets any better."

"What about the weather? Think it'll be like last winter?"

"Well, it's gonna be a terrible winter for the waterman. I can tell you that."

"How so?"

"Well, there's nothin' out there. Hasn't been for years."

"How'd you do today? Catch any good ones?"

"Not bad. I figger we'll all be rich by Christmas. Some o' them arsters are fat as pork. Course, some aren't so good—purty lean—and it's my guess we'll do good to break even."

"At least you're still at it, still going to go out again this year."

"Huh?"

"I say, things shouldn't be too bad. You're going out again this season."

"Well, there's a lot more to arsterin' than catchin' arsters."

Winter can leave Tilghman Island encased in ice so thick that even the swift moving, deep channel of Knapps Narrows where many workboats are moored cannot be navigated. Locked in the unmoving, silvern shroud of ice, the island and its tiny towns are uninterrupted by the shout of men and the rumble of diesels.

For some of the less frugal watermen, coping through the duration of a freeze-up is difficult. Pickup trucks and even their boats can go on sale. The bullet is bitten, and then gnawed. But their independent spirit prevails. During one harsh winter when ice prevented the catching of oysters, a fund drive was launched throughout the county to collect money for the most destitute watermen. Checks and cash were sent to the

JAMES DRAKE IAMS A.W.S. ©

islanders, but the munificence was turned down by the watermen. "All watermen know you have some bad times each year. You have to plan for it or suffer," was the collective reply.

When the ice breaks and workboats can be sailed to the oyster beds, the fleet comes alive with men eager for a catch and a retinue of gulls expostulating the reasons for any delay of activity.

Although the major harvest of Tilghman Island is seafood and there are a few little backyard gardens by the houses, it has a general reputation for reaping bumper crops of wild oats. It is said that in years past it was rather unwise for outsiders, and particularly blacks, to remain on the island after sundown when both the draw span over Knapps Narrows and a lot of hell could be raised. At times a number of young men, their confidence increased by a spirited group of supporters, loiter at the bridge guzzling beer and having a whooping good time to the chagrin of police and passersby. On at least one occasion a melee erupted with fists and epithets flying through the balmy summer evening. When police arrived and attempted to make arrests, a couple of revelers leaped off the bridge to make a watery escape.

For the most part, however, Tilghman Islanders conduct themselves with passive resistance to the outside. They, too, however, are realizing the value of the tourist trade and therefore offer excellent restaurants and productive charter fishing excursions for vacationers.

Once a year, traditionally in November after oyster season has been open for some time and there are plenty of oysters on the half shell, oysters steamed, and oyster fritters, Tilghman Islanders invite the public to cross over the drawbridge, observe the watermen's lifestyle and, perhaps, spend a little money while rubbing shoulders with the gum-booted, red-faced Islanders. For normally prosaic Tilghman Island, it is a grand state affair. Skipjacks are anchored in the narrows, shaft tongs are laid out in the parking lots for all to examine, those with artistic instincts display their latest works—

usually primitive oils of sailboats plowing through an aquamarine Bay or over-sized ducks skirting a canvas filled with brownish phragmites—and workboats are raced and docked for speed. Over nearly the entire island the chilly fall wind wafts the smells of barbequed chicken and fried clams and potatoes.

Tilghman watermen have been among the first to collectively acknowledge that their particular breed fascinates others. Although a close-knit lot, they are not arrogant. When an occasion calls for festivity, their quiet aloofness is dropped with ease.

Methods of catching oysters have varied little over the last several centuries, and the development of new ways has not necessarily meant the demise of the old. On any given day within the same area it is possible to see skipjacks under sail making "licks" over oyster beds, workboats rigged with hydraulic patent tongs plunging great steel rakes overboard, and in shallower waters men with shaft tongs prodding the oyster bars for a day's catch.

Talbot watermen, although decreasing in number, have been in the vanguard of finding other means of harvesting seafood from the Bay. It was a Talbot waterman who developed the mechanized clam rake that added another dimension to the regional commercial seafood industry. And recently in Talbot County some of the younger watermen have been donning wet suits and diving for oysters.

The success of these divers quieted skeptics who thought the murky waters of the Bay would prevent anyone from seeing what he was doing and that the near freezing temperatures of late winter would keep anyone from even entering the water.

Diving for oysters has become popular up and down the Bay. In some areas divers outnumber tongers, and the red flag with the white slash that must be flown from a boat while a diver is down is visible wherever workboats are seen.

With experience and luck, an oyster diver can accumulate his catch in less time than can a hand tonger. While the tonger must cull his oysters on board his boat, since he has no other way of separating legal and illegal sizes, the diver can eliminate this step by picking up the larger oysters.

Not all oystermen have been pleased by this new method of catching the bivalve. For safety reasons other vessels must stay clear of a boat flying the diver's flag. This

Anna McGarvey, *Tilghman Island*

means that tongers, who often work the same bar side-by-side with each other, are prohibited from catching oysters close to a diver. Legislators are attempting to designate boundaries which would keep tongers and divers apart.

Notwithstanding its classy knickknack shops and the thousands of camera-toting tourists who, breezing along Talbot's back roads, linger for a while on the serene banks of the Tred Avon River, Oxford makes many attempts not to be a stopover for rubbernecking daytrippers. Town residents consistently vote, in fact, against changes that would lure more free-spending visitors to the three-hundred-year-old community. They like it quite the way it is, thank you, those who own a share of the gem of Talbot, the village with brick-paved, tree-lined sidewalks, spanking-bright wooden houses, and narrow lanes that trail down to the water's edge.

Oxford claims only a handful of working watermen among its residents. The nearly five hundred boat slips are filled mostly with pleasure vessels piloted by a quiet breed who, besides injecting immense wealth into the area, do not make life difficult by living there year 'round.

Oxford is posh, at least in relative comparisons as other resort areas get tackier. It has not always been this way, however. For many years Oxford was nearly abandoned by the outside world as well as by the Shore. The dream of becoming the capital of the Eastern Shore faded towards the end of the eighteenth century. Oxford, a lively port, shipbuilding center, and county seat, was overgrown with weeds and stagnating with disuse. Ships traded elsewhere, and the seat of local government had been moved inland to Easton. But a century later the town stirred again, prodded by the construction of a rail line to its vicinity and by a commercial boom on the Delmarva peninsula. Oxford began to bustle once more. Shipments of crabs, oysters, grain, and tomatoes were redirected north to Wilmington and Philadephia instead of across the Bay by boat to Baltimore. New houses were built and families moved into the area.

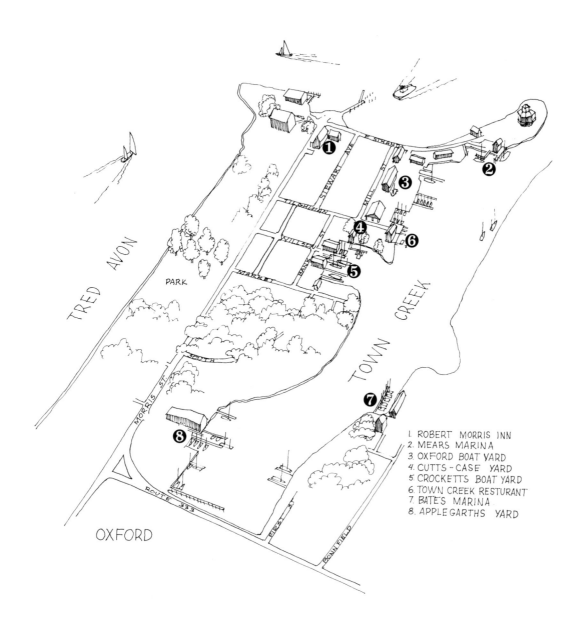

TRED AVON

PARK

TOWN CREEK

OXFORD

1. ROBERT MORRIS INN
2. MEARS MARINA
3. OXFORD BOAT YARD
4. CUTTS-CASE YARD
5. CROCKETTS BOAT YARD
6. TOWN CREEK RESTURANT
7. BATES MARINA
8. APPLEGARTHS YARD

And in this century Oxford has been discovered by the wealthy, leisure class of pleasure-minded families flush with the capital accumulated by their industrial parents and grandparents.

Oxford retains much of its turn-of-the-century atmosphere. And because its townspeople keep it trimmed and polished, Oxford draws those who wish for a few hours to throw off the heavy cloak of the "outside world" and to relax on The Strand as sailboats glide through and mallards dabble into the flat and glassy river.

Some of the finest boats to sail the Bay make their way up the Choptank River by the tiny fishing villages on Tilghman Island and into the Tred Avon. Oxford's location is easily spotted from the water; its towering water tank on the edge of Town Creek and the white-cabined car ferry growling back and forth across the Tred Avon from Oxford on the right to Bellevue on the left are unique in the region.

Oxford's boatyards have tended every type of boat that has sailed the Chesapeake. Applegarth's Marine Yard, perched snuggly with a sweeping vista of Town Creek cove, is often the temporary berth of skipjacks, varnished wooden speed boats, fiberglass-hulled yachts, cumbrous houseboats, and Bay-built workboats. Not far away, also on Town Creek, is the Oxford Boatyard. Its high sheds barely obscure a forest of masts and rigging on land and in water awaiting maintenance. Cutts and Case, formerly Wiley's Boatyard, is off Mill Street, half open to the wide sky and half shaded by tall trees. Some boat sheds have earth floors covered with wood shavings and sawdust. The air is rich in fumes of varnish and copper-laced bottom paint. Outside in the open yards vessels of many sizes and bulks rest on blocks. Boat bottoms with paint etched and dulled by sandbars and submerged tree trunks are exposed, making a novel sort of scenery. Yard employees with paint-speckled boots, blackened fingernails, and hats pulled down over matted hair move about with private determination. All in all, it is an untroubled air that envelopes the boatyards, and one without the slapdash opportunism so alien to Oxford.

Applegarth's Pier, Oxford

JAMES DRAKE IAMS A.W.S.

Among the bayside counties, Talbot gets the lion's share of the tourist dollar. Within Talbot County, St. Michaels is a principal attraction, a river town of thirteen hundred fulltime residents that burgeons during the summer months with many thousands more.

Halfway between Easton and Tilghman Island on Route 33, St. Michaels has shops, restaurants, and small houses waiting to be admired. And they are. Each year a quarter of a million people come to walk St. Michaels' streets and putter in its harbor. On a summery weekend every avenue, lane, and waterfront crawls with sightseers, many of them garbed in polo shirts, slacks, and deck shoes.

Tourists do not give the town a circus atmosphere, but one more resembling a low-key carnival or country fair. The pace is slow and activities decidedly alfresco.

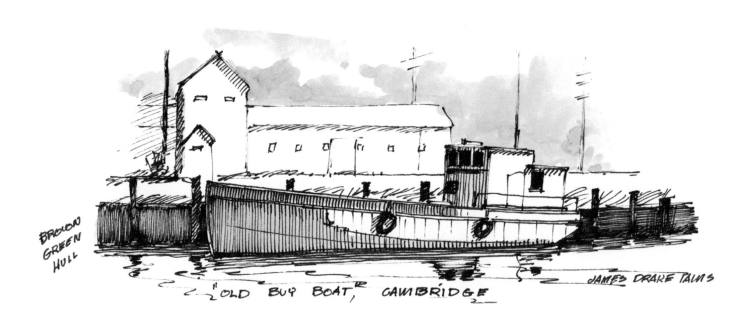

"OLD BUY BOAT," CAMBRIDGE

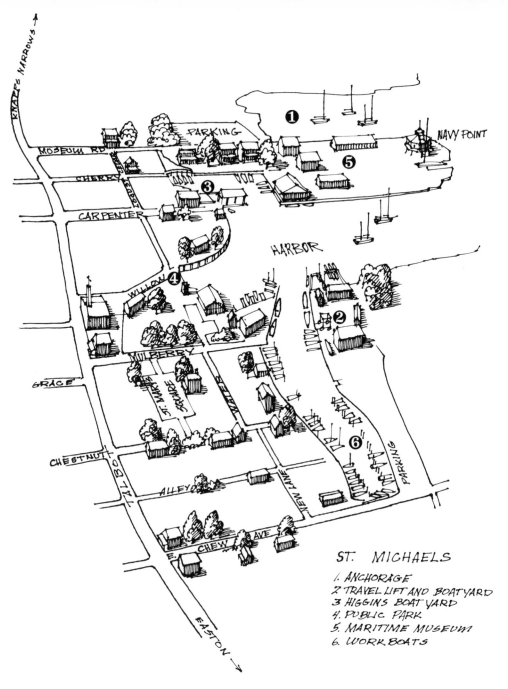

ST. MICHAELS

1. ANCHORAGE
2. TRAVEL LIFT AND BOATYARD
3. HIGGINS BOAT YARD
4. PUBLIC PARK
5. MARITIME MUSEUM
6. WORK BOATS

There is very little to do except walk or sit by the harbor, visit the Bay-oriented maritime museum, and eat and drink in the informal restaurants. But this limited itinerary is enough to satisfy many, for the number of tourists is increasing each season, and the tourist industry has become within the last decade the leading source of income.

Cherry Street, St. Michaels

JAMES DRAKE IAMS A.W.S. ©93

The long, low concrete bridge that spans the Choptank was brand new in the mid-thirties. Lately it has earned a disputable distinction of being one of the ten worst bridges in the nation. Its chipped stanchions and cracked pilings are evidence that motor vehicles and boats do not always stay in their lanes and channels. When there's an accident or when the draw span is raised to permit passage by a boat, traffic comes to a vibrating halt. If a portion of the bridge fell into the water, local residents would react with a "We-told-you-so" shrug. Some year a new bridge will be built over the Choptank, but exactly where is a matter of speculation since some opinion holds that it should cut through downtown Cambridge, thus bringing business to the merchants there, and some opinion has it that it should bypass the city to prevent traffic backups.

Cambridge has seen better days. The town was busy with the handling of commerce by land and by water. Boxcars and steamboats clanked and tooted strains of a healthy economy. Cambridge Creek, the heart of the city, was thick with workboats unloading seafood on the docks. Shipyards, a fertilizer plant, packing houses, and lumber mills hummed with enterprise. Pleasure boats were so numerous that there was not always space to dock them all in the yacht basin where Mill Street meets the river.

Cambridge was not spared the Shore's economic slump that lasted through the most recent decades. Unemployment, union troubles, and a conflagration of racial turmoil in the midsixties left Cambridge a weary and disillusioned river town.

Cambridge is beginning to see good days ahead. Pleasure boats are returning to a rebuilt yacht basin; sailboats and workboats are filling Cambridge Creek where luxury town houses have risen from the crumble of abandoned packing plants and sagging docks. Brick-lined High Street's bulky homes once again reflect the grandeur that was so evident at the beginning of the century.

Converted Buy Boat, Cambridge

The short ducking season of 1931 resulted in a crop of wildfowl during the season recently closed pleasantly reminiscent of the good old days when Maryland slaves complained of too much canvasback on the menu. Enormous rafts of redheads can still be seen from the shores of the bay and the music of the 'whiffler' is overheard. The abundance of this year only goes to prove that after all the wild duck is a hardy and prolific bird who, given half a chance, will endure despite automatic shotguns and baited blinds.

We who have been accustomed to plenty of wildfowl since the earliest days on this peninsula have something to worry about in the recent (Biological Survey) report. Figures show beyond a shadow of a doubt that the duck population is fast dwindling and the army of hunters is fast increasing. Those of us who returned empty handed last fall and winter manufactured all kinds of excuses for the scarcity of ducks. There was too much feed in the bay, the ducks are getting blind shy and all the rest of the reasons. But down in our hearts every one of us knew the sad truth—ducks were terribly scarce.

Newspaper readers on the Shore in the early 1930s, seeing these two editorial comments printed in the same paper within two years, must have been a bit puzzled over the contrasting reports. They were not the only ones perplexed by an on-again, off-again ducking season. Gunners, guides, watermen, game wardens, restaurant cooks, and farmers all scratched their heads over the perceptible changes in the size of the migratory bird population. Those less bothered by the scarcity, or unwilling to believe that one of the Shore's greatest traditions faced jeopardy, proposed reassuring theories for the absence of "enormous rafts" of ducks. When the winter was mild, ducks were finding plenty of food in the deeper, unfrozen regions of the Bay out of the gunner's sights. When winter was hard, ducks had migrated west where food was not so hard to find.

Federal wildlife officials had been calling for the unthinkable: closed seasons and smaller bag limits. Shore wardens scoffed at the suggestion. Ducks were hardy and

would come back in great numbers without government meddling. Besides, closing the season would be too much of a hardship on the guides and gunning club employees who desperately needed the income brought to the area by "sports" from Baltimore, Philadelphia, and New York City. Millions of dollars had been invested in waterfront improvements to make gunning more profitable; closing a season would be stealing future income from those who had risked their only stakes.

In 1935 the federal government adopted gunning regulations that stunned the Eastern Shore wildfowler. Sinkboxes and sneak boats were outlawed, as was the use of live decoys and shotguns larger than number ten gauge. A three-shell limit was placed on automatic and repeating shotguns. Bag limits were reduced to only ten ducks a day for each hunter. And no longer could the gunner who had slept through the morning count on getting his kill in late evening; the day's shoot was over when the sun went down.

Subsequent duck seasons improved little despite the new regulations. It is doubtful whether the Shore will ever see again ducks in pre-1930s numbers. Old heads who recall the days when waterfowl were so plentiful that only the breasts of the killed birds were eaten (the rest of the birds were tossed into the garbage or to the dogs; why eat wings and thighs when there were so many plump breasts to feast upon), accept that "those days are gone, boy."

Modest efforts, in addition to game regulations, were being made to ensure that waterfowl did not perish forever from the Shore. Most notable in these attempts was the quiet move in the early 1930s to set aside a portion of Dorchester's vast marshes as a wildlife refuge. The Blackwater River curls through the marsh some dozen miles south of Cambridge. The low, sodden land, inhabited by birds, reptiles, and small, fur-bearing mammals, was already a natural refuge of sorts. It included dense stands of loblolly pines, tall belts of reeds, open waters, and mud flats dappled with the tracks of muskrat and deer. The very nature of the marsh is pertinacious; even with some of man's improper meddling it remains thick with vegetation and flush with wildlife. So with man's intervention only occasionally to prevent unnatural disturbances, the marshland can be preserved.

Blackwater Refuge began with about eight thousand acres. Today it is nearly twice that in size. It is a major wintering area for ducks and Canada geese (the latter, the unofficial Shore bird, is relatively new to the area and was not seen in its current enormous numbers until the 1940s). Raccoons, otters, muskrats, deer, opossums, skunks, and even the red fox with a tail as long as its body make their home at Blackwater.

Blackwater is also the residence of the bald eagle. Its common perch is at the very top of a dead tree, shorn of bark and branches, where it has a tremendous overview of the marsh. A narrow hardtop road cuts through the refuge. Normally at least one eagle is within sight of the road and photographers who might never have the opportunity anywhere else can take rolls of shots of an eagle here.

The practice of banding waterfowl indicates that each year many of the same birds migrate to the refuge. While a cornfield less than a mile away may be without a single Canada goose, for example, the refuge teems with them.

JAMES DRAKE IAMS A.W.S. ©83

In western shore restaurants and private kitchens diners may prefer to call the dish marsh rabbit. But the euphemism cannot disguise the oily taste or hide the fact that the dark meat patted in flour and fried in grease is plain old muskrat from the marsh.

Muskrat trapping is as traditional as oystering in this part of the Shore, although the demand for the meat and pelt and the scarcity of the 'rat seldom combine to make it a full-time occupation. Trappers have a two-fold interest in muskrats. The skins can be sold for between five and ten dollars (the black muskrats are prized as "money 'rats"), and the meat can be eaten as a dividend or sold through the local country store.

Muskrats are legally trapped only during the coldest months of the year. Two types of trap are most common: the pedal or jump trap and the boxlike Conibear trap set off by a trigger mechanism bumped by the animal as it crawls into the cage. The Conibear trap is thought by some to be more humane because it can kill the animal instantly. It does have the drawback of being set off by twigs and ducks floating through its wire frame.

The jump trap is the model that outrages owners of pets who live near the marshes. It is set off when weight is applied to a pedal, releasing two metal bridges that snap together with tremendous pressure. Although the clamps are without teeth, they hold the animal's limb tightly and in a struggle to get free, the hapless prisoner can easily mangle its leg. Trappers claim that muskrats can survive the injuries of the pedal trap if they manage to pull free, and sometimes even when they leave a limb behind. 'Rats with but three legs and a nicely healed stump have been caught. Usually the captured animal is discovered dead.

Old-head trappers used a method called "gigging" to kill muskrats. This required only that the individual own a pole with a barbed prong, possess the knowledge of discerning what was a muskrat mound and what was simply a clump of marsh grass, and bear the nature to kill an animal at close range. Once a 'rat mound was discovered, the trapper would lean down to examine its surface. Even on very chilly mornings, a cluster of muskrats sleeping within the mound would raise enough heat to cause frost and ice to melt. If the trapper saw that this was the case, he stabbed at the nest with the gig, killing, maiming, or at least panicking the family within.

Trappers, when called upon to do so, will defend the killing of muskrats with determination. The 'rats, they say, are enemies of the marsh and of farmland that borders creeks and ponds. The 'rats burrowing causes the drainage of water and a general weakening of the shoreline. If they were not caught, the prolific breeders would overrun the tidewater terrain. And, in a subtle twist of logic, the 'rats must be harvested in the interest of the fur business, for they tend to inbreed and grow inferior pelts.

It is less common today to find muskrat served outside a Shoreman's home. The meat, which tastes much like terrapin, is not in great demand any more. But when it is sold "over the counter" for cooking, state laws require that the head and feet be kept intact to ensure that the buyer realizes what he or she is paying for.

To the west of central Dorchester, past the expanses of Kentuck Swamp, Buttons Neck, Russell Swamp, and Raccoon Creek Marsh, lies a fragile coastline of more soggy soil, inhabited by heron, muskrat, and waterman. Tiny fishing hamlets of less than a dozen homes and businesses have been here for centuries, yet they have never shed their precarious air. Any moment it seems they might silently slip into the encroaching Bay and not be discovered missing until the arrival of spring's sport fishermen.

Once a great duck hunting area (homes on Hooper Island had iron bars fixed outside the second-story windows to prevent ducks from crashing through the panes), the region is an end-of-the-earth domain of solitude. Everything there appears to be in a conspiracy to give its remoteness the fullest effect. There are countless little coves with small workboats tied to pine poles. Abandoned houses lean but a few degrees from falling completely over. In yards are neat stacks of crab pots and not-so-neat parking arrangements of junked cars and pickups. The occasional country store may or may not be open. A few packing houses hold claim on most of the activity, and that is in the form of idling boats at dockside and idling refrigerated trucks on the shell-covered parking lot.

There are some signs of affluency—new radar units atop boat cabins, mobile homes set upon clean concrete blocks, a repaved stretch of road here and there—but in many places the latest fixtures are "for sale" signs.

This could be Chessie country. Chessie is the Bay's version of the serpent that purportedly inhabits the deep waters of Loch Ness in Scotland. Reported sightings of Chessie have been increasing lately; not long ago a man looked from his house on Kent Island's bayside shore and spotted what he believed to be a twenty- to thirty-foot object undulating in the water. He grabbed his home video camera, raced onto the beach, and caught a few seconds of the scene on film. No one has verified that what is dark and moving and long on the film actually was a sea serpent in the Bay. The speculation it provoked was enjoyed by many, however, and a number of other "witnesses" claimed Chessie is fond of surfacing in the Bay near the ship channel off Dorchester County. (In the 1920s on Smith Island down the Bay several miles a waterman said he found the inverted, shed skin of a snake some twenty feet in length. The skin was discovered caught on some marsh grass. At that time it was proposed that a large jungle snake had somehow been carried into the Bay undetected aboard a ship returning from South America, and that the reptile had slipped into the waters off Smith Island before finding its way ashore.)

The Lower Shore is poultry country, and Route 50 passes dozens of long chicken houses where millions of broilers are raised and then trucked in a flurry of feathers off the Shore. On a steamy summer day the predominant smell over the highway is either the odor from the chicken houses or the tempting smell of barbequed chicken. Smokey

JAMES DRAKE JAMS A.W.S.

clouds pour from charcoal pits set up alongside the highway by civic and church clubs huckstering chicken to the beach-bound motorists.

During the depression era, when the broiler industry was small but chicken houses were nevertheless numerous on the Lower Shore, chicken stealing was a moderately popular nighttime activity within some circles. Live chickens, it seemed, were nearly as good as paper currency. They could be traded for other goods—shoes, vegetables, tobacco, a pint of moonshine—and if they could not be spent in such a way, they at least could be cooked and eaten.

Since chickens are light sleepers and easily become alarmed, stealing the birds without the immediate knowledge of their owner is not the easy task one may imagine, unless, that is, the thief practiced stealth and followed a few rudimentary, homespun

methods. Depending largely upon the weather, a chicken thief needed only two or three readily available items: a broom handle, a boiled Irish potato, and a burlap bag.

If the night air was cool, the broom handle was quite effective. The thief rubbed the length of stick as he neared the chicken house so that the friction between wood and the palm of his hand produced heat. The handle was held out in front of the roost and very slightly against the chicken's feet. The bird, sensing the warmth of the broom handle even though asleep, would step onto the stick. The thief then gingerly carried the chicken outside (this method worked best when stealing fowl sleeping close to one of the chicken house doors) and dumped it off the handle and into the burlap bag.

If the weather was hot or if the thief was not certain he could carry a chicken away without it waking with a giveaway squawk, the boiled Irish potato (pronounced "ash tater") came in handy. The thief, carrying the potato in one hand, approached the chicken from behind. When but a foot or two away, he would grab the chicken by the neck with his free hand and jam the startled bird's beak into the potato. If done with some expertise, the ensuing sounds were the flapping of a surprised chicken's wings and the closing of the chicken house door.

Most farmers in the area are aware of the benefits gotten from a coexistence with the common blacksnake. The blacksnake may be the farmer's best mouse and rat catcher, so normally the snake is tolerated around barns and grain storage tanks. But what does a chicken farmer do when he discovers too many chicks and eggs missing and he prefers not to kill every blacksnake he comes upon? One Lower Shore farmer devised a plan of ridding his chicken house of the unwanted reptile while leaving the others unharmed. He selected a nest that had been robbed repeatedly, and into it he placed a solid wooden oval similar in size and shape to a chicken egg. He checked the nest the following day and discovered that the bogus egg was gone. When he soon after came upon a blacksnake with a suspicious bulge in its center, the farmer killed the snake, ridding himself of a minor problem and the snake of a major misery.

JAMES DRAKE IAMS A.W.S. ©82

72   BAYSIDE IMPRESSIONS

Wicomico County

For the unhurried traveler, it is often the road least taken that holds the greatest rewards. On the Shore, as elsewhere, the road least taken is the secondary route that breaks away from the major highway and meanders through the countryside as though designed along the path of a stray but insouciant dog. Indeed, there are occasions when one wonders if the sole reason for ever laying some of these roads was to lure the harried motorist from the blacktop mainstream to areas mollified with wide cornfields, pine woods, and little villages no bigger than their zip codes. There are a number of such roads branching away from busy Route 50. Following one or two for half an hour can lead to some pleasant discoveries.

In Wicomico County, Route 347 is the first leg of a particularly diverting mini-journey. Meeting Route 50 half a dozen miles northeast of Salisbury, the narrow road first leads to the quiet town of Hebron, quite visible but very detached from the major highway. Hebron is a blend of small houses—most with neat yards—and an unobtrusive business section. The prevailing physical feature of the town, like many other Shore towns of a similar size, is the lofty metal water tower. Its huge holding tank, capped with a cylindrical roof, resembles the oversized head of some early Hollywood director's vision of a mechanical man. At the southern end of Hebron, past a row of white-walled and green-roofed houses, is a small carnival grounds. Four or five amusement rides are set up in place throughout the year, although they are activated but a few times.

Several miles south of Hebron is Quantico, a subdued, one-street hamlet marked at one end by a Methodist church and at the other end by an Episcopal church. Between the two are a number of houses worthy of taking a place on any of the fine streets in some of the Shore's wealthier communities. There is only one gravestone in the Methodist churchyard, and a chunk of marble signifying the site of a buried tricentennial time capsule to be unearthed and its contents revealed in the year 2076. At the opposite end of town, on all four sides of the yard surrounding the Episcopal church, are scores of gravestones evenly divided between Methodists and Episcopalians. Why both congregations choose to inter their dead in the same yard is not outwardly apparent. But then there is no apparent reason why they should not.

Route 347 meets Route 349 a mile south of Quantico. Traveling west one encounters Bivalve, Nanticoke, and Waterview; their names indicate their proximity to the water. Turning east on Route 349 and then south onto Route 352 leads to one of the Shore's best kept secrets—the unpretentious ferry town of Whitehaven.

By 1992 the ferry at Whitehaven will have been in operation for three hundred years. But it is doubtful that there will be much fanfare paid to the occasion. The villagers on the Wicomico River do not appear to be inclined toward grand state affairs. There are no brassy festivals, carnivals, or fairs in Whitehaven as there are in most other bayside communities up and down the Shore. Red-letter days—those celebrations touted by residents to draw tourists to their towns—simply do not exist on the Whitehaven calendar. But in a sense every day in Whitehaven is a red-letter day. Couched between fringes of green marsh before the wide Wicomico and below a full, outstretched sky, the village is a silent exclamation of the healing solitudes of the Lower Shore.

Back Creek, Hooper Island

Excepting for the periodic drone of the dieseled cable ferry as it lurches across the river, Whitehaven is without a cynosure of activity. Most of the working residents commute by automobile to Salisbury or to Princess Anne (only the latter use the ferry to reach their jobs). The boatyard at the southern end of town usually is quiet, and what movement does take place there is shielded by a curtain of tall reeds. There are no commercial businesses to speak of in Whitehaven, and the hulking structure that was the hotel on the northern side of town is closed. Midway between the boatyard and the hotel on the waterfront is a small, one-room shed by the docks where ice cream and soft drinks sometimes are sold, but only during summer months.

Reed Grass

DARK RED

STRIP PLANKED BOAT

Whitehaven is laid out in a triangle of narrow lanes. Whitehaven Road and Church Street form one angle; they fork to meet the ends of River Road at the water. Houses line the streets. Backyard flower gardens bloom in the spring. Behind one of the houses, unseen by the passerby, a wind chime clinks in the breeze, and the casual melody can be the most distinct sound of the moment. Short driveways are covered with bright oyster shells. Songbirds flit from yard to yard. Atop a forty-foot stand that once held high a windmill is fixed a television antenna.

Along River Road there are ten houses, all facing the water. Some are freshly painted; others are paint-bare and boarded up. But the contrast is not aesthetically displeasing. The waterfront is pricked with piers which, like the houses near them, are in various stages of repair. There are a few boats tied here and there. One or two may be filled with pine stakes and fishnet, as though someone had intended to set them out but found another, less taxing, activity to do. In the water near the abandoned hotel is the moored Coast Guard lightship *Frying Pan*, towed up the Wicomico several years ago from its post off the Carolinas. At the other end of the waterfront a rusting trawler is nested in the mud. Each vessel is pointed toward the other. In their arrangement they appear as guardians of the town, inappropriate but benign hulks of scrap metal.

Across the river from Whitehaven and half-submerged in the dark water are two rotting wooden barges—perches for a dozen gulls whose activity rivals that of the village on the far shore.

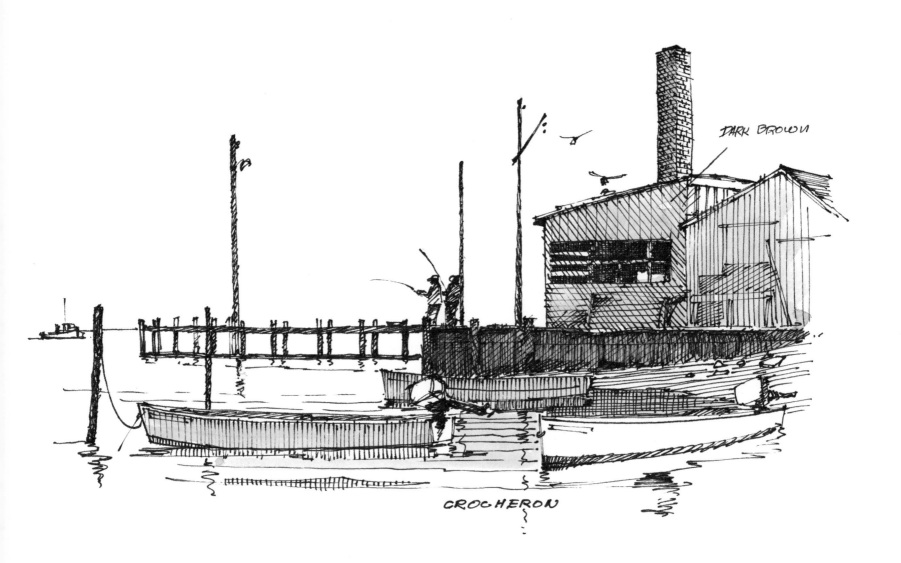

DARK BROWN

CROCHERON

Crocheron

HIGGIN'S BOAT YARD

Somerset County

The fourteen slumbery miles of Maryland Route 413 leading south into Somerset County's lowland and ultimately to Crisfield make up what surely is the straightest hardtop thoroughfare on the Eastern Shore. At times the fourteen miles pass like forty. In summer the road's thin horizon dances with heat waves; during winter's early dark evenings the drive is black and tedious.

Through stands of loblolly pines, by fields created with the clearing of trees, and past small frame houses, the highway dips to a region where land and Bay meet without bank or wave.

Crisfield is the southernmost incorporated town not only on the Shore, but in the whole of Maryland. Directly across the Bay is the mouth of the Potomac River and the beginning of Virginia's tidewater region. Less than five miles south of Crisfield are the Virginia waters of Pocomoke Sound.

If the Chesapeake rises again, as some say it will, to a prehistoric level, Crisfield and its environs will be the first of the mainland reclaimed by water. The water table is so high, it is said locally with the customary straight face, that digging a well requires that dirt be trucked in. Unlike the Upper Shore with its higher elevation and clay banks, bayside Somerset is soaked with brine and its shoreline changes with every tidal hour.

Vegetation able to survive the burning saltiness of the water and soil grows thick. The land is blanketed with sedge grass and cordgrass, myrtle bush, and sassafras. Wherever the earth rises a few feet, brush and loblollies, reeds, and wide, wild cherry trees thrive. Atop ditch banks bunches of asparagus (pronounced colloquially as "spargras") grow in midspring, and from the depths of the ditches shoot razor-sharp reeds.

Crisfield is one of the youngest towns along the Shore's coast. As the modest and lonely fishing village of Somers Cove, it was shrouded for decades in the quietude of sea breezes and crying gulls. A post-Civil War passion in the north for the oyster, and especially for the tangy lower Bay oyster, transformed the hamlet into a raucous community of several thousand inhabitants and transients eager to earn a living off the rich oyster beds abundant just offshore in Tangier and Pocomoke sounds. Money was to be made in the catching and shucking of the bivalve, or from those who caught and shucked. Soon the Chesapeake blue crab was added to the commercial seafood industry; Crisfield was destined to become the "seafood capital of the world," its early publicists predicted.

Pilings were driven into the soft mud around the cove and out into the water. Planking was nailed down so that access could be made to navigable depths. Wooden shanties, shucking and packing houses, saloons, banks, theaters, churches, warehouses, stores, and rows of houses were erected in a short time. Boatyards expanded, as did sail lofts and foundries. A barrel factory was built to meet the demand for shipping containers.

The town of Somers Cove, now much more than a quiet village, was renamed Crisfield in honor of the entrepreneur responsible for having the railroad line extended south from Salisbury and Princess Anne to the busy harbor, right up to the main wharf so that in some cases seafood was unloaded from the boat and into the boxcar.

Evening, Deal Island

JAMES DRAKE IAMS A.W.S. © 83

Quite literally, Crisfield expanded out onto the narrow inlets and small guts about the cove where millions of bushels of oyster shells had been dumped, forming what must be one of the most unusual foundations ever devised for urban sprawl.

No fewer than three fires devastated large portions of Crisfield's business section; particularly affected was the wharf area. Town leaders passed an ordinance stipulating that no longer would any new structure be built of wood. One- and two-story concrete and brick buildings were to replace those lost in the fires. That no one set of architect's plans was followed in the designing of the buildings is apparent because the facades of the stores and warehouses lining the street leading down to the wharf greet the passerby like a gauntlet of sideshow countenances, none belonging to the same family, but all akin, nevertheless, through a benign freakishness.

While Crisfield may be the chronological toddler of the bayside communities, it retains more than any other harbor town the character of those turn-of-the-century boom days when the coins of the realm were oyster and crab and terrapin, and when those who lived there believed there was an opportunity to pocket a share of the new wealth.

The appropriate sounds and smells of a working water town can be expected in Crisfield each season: the early morning whine of pickup truck tires driving on otherwise silent streets, the popping and sputtering of diesel engines as workboats move in and out of the harbor, the smell of oyster shells piled high outside shucking houses, and in summer, when the town is often without a breeze, the unmistakable, pervasive aroma of steamed crabs.

There remains in Crisfield a rather dinsome band of watermen and packing house workers, naturally sullied by their trades and slightly troubled by their cut of the profits. When the harvest is going well (prices are high and supply is moderate), the town stays awake late. The several bars are filled with customers, and the food markets are active with women and children. High school-age youths drive the main streets to a redundant point. Watermen from Tangier Island and Smith Island stay on the mainland until dark. When the local economy is ebbing (supply of seafood is either too low or too high), the town grows silent with the arrival of dusk.

The remoteness of Crisfield from the major east-west highways and from metropolitan Salisbury enables it to continue its customs in language and behavior. Moreover, those who move to Crisfield from other parts tend to change to Crisfield ways. Elsewhere on the Shore, the towns have changed with the influx of outsiders until they are an amalgam of Eastern Shore and Baltimore and Philadelphia. In Crisfield, colloquialisms, accent, and centuries-old customs are as much a part of the area today as is the sandy soil.

The influence upon speech and mannerisms by the community's elderly residents—the "old heads"—is strong. The young waterman may have hair to his shoulders, wear white rubber boots, and tune his radio to contemporary music, but his language and knowledge of the water is that of his forefathers. Even if he does not always speak it, he knows that a "tippet" is the last part of a chicken to cross over a fence, that when he's "pethy" he wishes he brought more to eat aboard his boat, and that his "gumboots" should keep him from falling on a slippery deck and breaking his "krumper" bone.

Through disaster and hard times Crisfielders have developed a brand of humor spiced with dark optimism and unabashed exaggeration. When the temperature is high, "it's never been this hot," and when the ice is thick on Tangier Sound, "it's never been so thick." Someone reacting to a bit of bad luck has a "frown as long as a trotline." And working on the water "can make a man a small fortune. Providing he starts out with a big one."

Poverty—especially distant poverty—is a badge of honor. "We was so poor when I was a boy," goes an expression borrowed from vaudeville days, "that all we had to eat was crackers. We had to wipe our bottoms with a whisk broom."

Expressions of speech evolving from times lost are used commonly. "Tough as Dennard's bull" is spoken by someone having trouble, perhaps, cutting a piece of meat, who never knew Dennard and certainly never saw his bull.

Physical features of acquaintances are described and tolerated casually as fundamental parts of a conversation. "So-and-so stopped in t'other day. You know him. He's the one with buck teeth so bad he could eat the last kernel of corn out of a funnel."

Also from physical appearances or from individual mannerisms or from incidents that happened long ago come nicknames used more widely than birth names. For example: Sour Belly, Fleabait, Tincan, Jimmy Marble, Firespike, Iron Tail, Greenleaf, Hendonkey, and Scowlhead.

The man who decides to stay "on the water" knows that few things in his life are more important than his workboat, and that much of what he earns will go to its upkeep. Today's workboats, wooden or fiberglass, carry price tags into the tens of thousands of dollars. Outfitting one with electronic equipment, patent tongs for oystering or a rig for clamming, crab pots, spare diesel engine parts, as well as renting a boat slip, and keeping the fuel tanks filled takes as much money as it does to start a small business. In fact, with the boat owner responsible for keeping his own records, hiring helpers, keeping tabs on the market, and, above all else, making sure that his boat stays afloat, the waterman is a small businessman. The daily routine of affairs connected with working on the water dilutes some of the romanticism normally ascribed to the waterman. He's not likely to take the family for a boat ride on his day off.

Several decades ago a government customs house was located in the center of Crisfield. Housed in a wing of the post office, the customs house was a bustling place. Boats registered in Crisfield numbered in the thousands and included nearly every type. The boats in the harbor at day's end were so crowded that one could walk on decks from one shore to the other without getting wet. Crisfield's small drawbridge—a

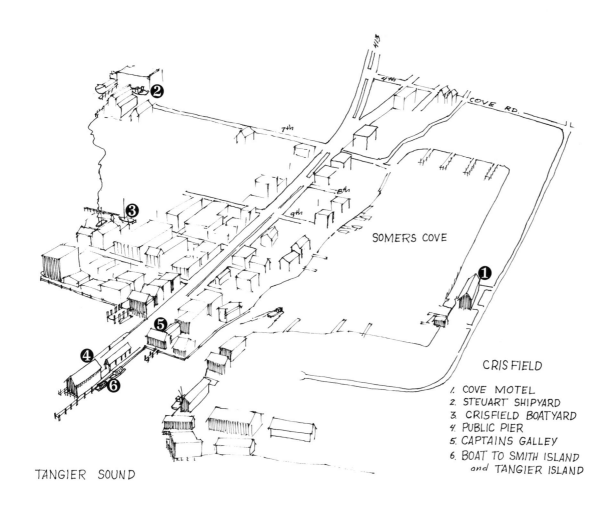

SOMERS COVE

CRISFIELD

1. COVE MOTEL
2. STEUART SHIPYARD
3. CRISFIELD BOATYARD
4. PUBLIC PIER
5. CAPTAINS GALLEY
6. BOAT TO SMITH ISLAND *and* TANGIER ISLAND

TANGIER SOUND

bridge that actually was pulled or drawn back onto the land to let boats pass—linking the town to the packing houses on Jersey Island across the channel finally was dismantled because it was more often open than closed. A creek was filled in nearby and a road was made onto Jersey so that technically it no longer is an island.

The number of boats in Crisfield has diminished greatly and the customs house office has been relocated in Baltimore. Still, more workboats are to be found here than in any other harbor on the Shore. Watermen from other counties as far north as Kent sail to Crisfield and work the local waters for crabs, oysters, and, most recently, clams. Crisfield boats seldom venture far from the area. Occasionally, when the catch is poor in Tangier Sound and it is reported that the situation is better in Virginia waters, a Crisfielder will sail south. Crossing the state line to catch seafood is unlawful, and the incidents of gunfire exchanged between Marylanders and Virginians are real, not legend.

Most of Crisfield's commercial fleet tie up in what is called the Little Boat Harbor (as opposed to the larger harbor of Somers Cove), located on the northwest side of town in a well-protected, dredged inlet off the Little Annemessex River. The harbor is out of sight from the main street through Crisfield and to get there by land one must take the side streets through neighborhoods of neat houses and trimmed lawns.

Some workboats are docked in Somers Cove, but this harbor is increasingly taken over by pleasure and sport boaters. The cove has been dredged and landscaped, and hundreds of new slips have been built. It is one of the finest bayside harbors on the Chesapeake. When summer gales whip the waters of Tangier Sound to a froth, Somers Cove is a "slick ca'm," as the expression goes.

The Ward brothers, Lem and Steve, grew up during the teens of this century in the Calvary district just outside Crisfield. Their father, Trav, was an on-again, off-again shipwright who built a number of thirty-foot skipjacks in the yard beside the Ward house. When he wasn't swinging his axe or hammer about the boat frames, or shucking oysters in town for twenty cents a gallon, or leading the choir at the Asbury Methodist Church, Trav was the neighborhood barber.

"Uncle Trav," as he was known by the Calvary youngsters, built a one-room barbershop beside the straight road leading directly to the Jenkins Creek boat landing. The shop was in a plain little building with less than two hundred square feet of floor space. Sunlight entered through two windows, one in the front and another in the rear. Four plank steps rose to the only door. The building was also of wood, and on the sharply pitched roof was a short brick stack. There were some modest curls of trim at the front of the shop just below the roof crown. When the building was freshly painted a popcorn yellow, it would glow with the reflection of the sun-bleached oystershell road that lay before it.

Like most structures in the area, Trav's barbershop was set on a foundation that raised it above the ground and above the level of the occasional flood tide that covered Calvary in a foot of salt water. Beneath the shop Lem and Steve discovered a refreshing deliverance from the summer heat. They would crawl into the dark and cool space and lie on their backs listening to the scuffle of feet across the wooden floorboards above their faces.

The barbershop served as a gathering place for the local men. There they would swap gunning and fishing stories and talk of the weather, all the while taking tobacco in the form of cigarettes, chaw, and snuff.

There were two long mirrors on the walls and a few shelves upon which rested shaving mugs and containers of lather, powder, and tonic. Hot towels were pulled from a bright copper steamer. Nearby hung a Regulator clock. Two framed prints, tacked to the wall facing the barber chairs, were Trav's only attempt at interior decoration. One was a portrait of Teddy Roosevelt, and the other a pen-and-ink drawing of a comely woman. She wore a high-collared, long dress which she lifted slightly, revealing a delicate ankle, as she carefully crossed a muddy street. Her eyes were fixed to the dark clouds overhead, and she spoke to a young boy sitting on the curb. "I'd very much like to see it clear up," she remarked in handwritten script at the bottom of the print. The boy, his eyes riveted on her ankle, replied, "I'd sure like to see it clear up, too."

Lem and Steve, following the movements of Trav as he worked on his own rig, carved their first decoys in the little barbershop. It was much cheaper to make their own decoys, and since ducks were so plentiful and could be lured to almost anything that resembled a bird, an entire gunning rig could be finished in the spare time during the summer months before the waterfowl migrated to the area.

Sometime after Steve returned to Calvary from France where he had served in the United States Army at the close of World War I, the Ward brothers formed a carving and painting team and turned out thousands of decoys for local hunters as well as the wealthy sportsmen drawn to lower Somerset by the prospects of a good shoot. Among decoy collectors the Ward product is the best known. Ward birds, which sold for a few dollars a pair and have been burned in wood stoves by hunters when the firewood supply became exhausted, are now museum and mantel pieces valued at several thousand dollars each.

Waterfront, Crisfield

The barbershop served also as the decoy shop. Both brothers reluctantly continued cutting "suits of hair," and when they had no customers, they hacked and carved and painted until the room smelled more of turpentine than aftershave lotion and hair tonic.

Trav's barbershop was moved fifteen yards back from the road. Lem and Steve had two rooms added onto the shop—one on each end—and a new front was built so that the three-roomed building looks as if it were built at the same time. There are no outward signs that the shop was that of the highly respected brothers, but cars and buses filled with admirers of the Ward brothers and their decoys find their way down the narrow Calvary roads to the shop where they stop for a moment, and then drive on.

Of the two brothers, Lem did most of the fine carving and feather painting. Steve rough cut the bodies and heads, first with a hatchet and then, with more deliberate

'Round chine'

'Hard chine'

strokes, he used smaller carving knives. Both brothers loved to recite poetry, particularly the kind of poetic confections popular among newspaper readers of the day. Steve wrote his own verse, modeling his style after writers such as James Whitcomb Riley and Robert Service, and mailed his pieces off to the papers for publication. Many were printed locally, and he received praise from readers who saw some of his poems in the western shore papers. Steve only wrote about that which he knew best, so the subject of nearly every one of his poems is Crisfield, as in "The Crisfield Oyster Fleet":

> They are fixing up the skipjacks and the canoes by the score,
> And the runboats jam the railways 'til there's room for not one more.
> They are rigging up the batteaus and the bugeyes white and neat
> As September brings a greeting to the Crisfield oyster fleet.
>
> There's new tongs and culling hammers, new ropes all bright and strong,
> There's new things of ev'ry manner, and in each heart a brand new song.
> They are ready, they are waiting for old Tangier's tasty treat
> As September sings a greeting to the Crisfield oyster fleet.
>
> From the many inland rivers soon you'll hear the motors hum
> Through the stillness of the evenings, loaded down as home they come.
> For it's oyster time in Tangier and in Pocomoke's broad sweep
> When September smiles a greeting to the Crisfield oyster fleet.

The mouth of Jenkins Creek is bridged by an arch of timber and concrete. At the highest point Lawsonia Marsh is plainly visible. Several thousand yards away the cherry trees and shrubs mark the entrance to Broad Creek. Beyond that is Cedar Island Marsh, once the site of much of Somerset County's finest duck hunting.

At the northern foot of the bridge is a crab shanty built over the creek. Beyond it are more shanties. Some are linked to the marsh by walkways; others stand unattached. One shanty has been built atop a half-sunken buy boat. There are perhaps a dozen such shanties on Jenkins Creek. At one time there were many more, and when the masted workboats were moored and evening was nearing an end, the horizon looked like a burned-out pine forest.

On the north side of Jenkins Creek and inside the bight formed by two lanes leading to the bridge was a neighborhood store under the management of Jim ("Brinks") Nelson. The white houses scattered here and there on the edge of the marsh constituted what was called the brinks community, since it was located on the brink of the water and mud.

Brinks' country store was one of a few in Calvary and Byrdtown, on the other side of the creek, and there was enough business to keep the stores going until the late fifties when one-stop markets were built in Crisfield. The old stores are empty now, their roofs leak, and vines grow through glassless window frames. Brinks' store has been converted into a home. And in case someone returns to Crisfield after an absence of three decades and decides to drive down to the landing to see if any acquaintances are at Brinks', there is a "Closed" sign displayed prominently, even though the building has not served as a store in more than a decade.

Country stores such as the one by the Jenkins Creek boat landing served a valuable social function in earlier days. Next to the church, the store was the center of gatherings. Late evenings in the store usually were reserved for the men who strolled down to their boats for a final scrutiny or repair. They would stop by the store, drink a bottle of beer or two, smoke their cigarettes, and discuss the political and economic weather. Shenanigans were not uncommon. The men frequenting Brinks' place were sometimes rough, but the nightly episodes there seldom went beyond the rogueries of worn watermen, small-time bootleggers, and amateur pugilists. For example, one incident that occurred at Brinks' store goes something like this: The sun had set and the

Skipjack, Deal Island

James Drake Iams A.W.S. ©83

winds from the south shifted to a chilly nor'easterly when a group of men gathered inside. Someone stoked the wood stove and the others dragged chairs and wooden boxes around and settled down for an evening's worth of conversation. A few minutes passed by and one fellow, dissatisfied by the lack of spirited dialogue, stood up and casually announced his belief that a stick of dynamite without a cap or fuse could not explode even if it were tossed into a fire.

The resultant skepticism was loud and jeering. Realizing that he was the only advocate of this theory, the fellow reached into a back pocket and for all to see produced a single stick of dynamite. The ridicule continued, so he stepped toward the wood stove and unlatched its door to reveal a sizzling fire. The room grew quiet and all eyes were upon the fist wrapped tightly around the explosive.

Tension was at its peak when, with a quick flick of his wrist, the man sent the dynamite into the blaze. Chairs and boxes were overturned in the scramble to open windows and the front door of the store. It was chest against back as the men collectively struggled for distance between themselves and the stove. But in the crescendo of yelps and whoops there was an unexpected silence. The dynamite did not explode, and the only man who did not move from where he had been standing was smiling with great satisfaction. His point had been made: without a detonation cap or a fuse, a stick of dynamite in a fire is as harmless as an oyster in a chamber pot.

There is one method, standing at water's edge almost anywhere on the Shore, to determine if one is north or south of, say, Kent Island: survey the salt marsh. If it covers only several acres or less and lies within a wide-mouthed ravine, or if its edge rises quickly to a hummock thick with pines and shrubs, chances are good that the Bay bridges linking Kent Island and the western shore are to the south. If the marsh is wider than the fixed horizontal range of the eye and is so reticulated with channels that it is impossible to walk fifty yards in a straight path, it is very likely that Kent Island is to the north.

Although the entire Shore appears to be tabletop flat, the land actually shelves downward from north-northeast to south-southwest. The farther down the Shore one travels, the flatter it becomes. Marshes are spread over hundreds and hundreds of acres. Much of the coastline is soggy mud and sand held together by the meshing of plant roots, the combination of earth and vegetation being in most cases the only deterrent to erosion.

Lower Somerset County is as marshy as the Shore ever gets. Land developers, scratching their heads in an effort to discover a way of making the vast expanses of land suitable for home construction, are stymied. Wetlands are virtually uninhabitable by humans.

Low tide in the salt marsh makes for a pungent few hours; exposed mud releases the gases of marsh life and death. The smell is almost sweet. But for the heavy traces of decaying plant and marine life, it would be a peculiar, natural kind of perfume. (It is not surprising that upon gutting a waterfowl that has fed on the roots and minnows found in the marsh, an identical odor rises from the innards.)

Marsh gas, at times heavy over the flats or "mud heads," can drift within thin, moist bubbles up and across the land. Called jack-o'-lanterns by some of the watermen, these ghostly formations create an eerie scene at night as they float along, wobbling grayish reflections of the moon. It is claimed that duck hunters unfamiliar with the phenomenon have attempted to follow these fragile globes through the pathless marsh until their concentration was interrupted by a knee-deep plunge into a creek or sink hole.

Other, immensely more bothersome products of the marsh spring forth each late spring. Biting insects—greenheads, deerflies, and mosquitoes—are as plentiful today as they were decades ago when many of the wetlands were drained to destroy their breeding grounds.

Compared with its Upper Shore cousin (which is nothing more than a naggish bijou of a bug), the salt-marsh mosquito of the lower counties is brutal, ruthless, and seemingly on the earth for the single purpose of irritating warm-blooded creatures. A quick plunge with its fiery sucker and the mosquito leaves its human victim with a solid welt and a week's worth of scratching.

Backyard summer picnics in this tidewater terrain are short affairs. Before the advent of insect repellent, smudge pots of burning oil-soaked rags were used to lay a smoke screen to give diners some respite from the insect attacks.

Tales have it that outside Crisfield a cow managed to break its rope tether and wandered from a yard into the marsh in search of food. The cow, breathing heavily from its laborious movements through the mud, inhaled so many of the insects that it suffocated before a distraught owner could steer it out of the marsh.

Year after year the state tries to combat the mosquito with poisons sprayed from airplanes swooping down over the marshes and from trucks, mounted with cannonlike devices, driving through the countryside showering the ditches with pesticide.

Just below Crisfield harbor, cupping the mouth of Jenkins Creek as it converges with the Little Annemessex, is the expansive Cedar Island Marsh. Bayside it is sandy, with long, gleaming strips of sand strewn with plastic bottles and styrofoam markers torn by wind or boat propeller from crab pots set out in Tangier Sound. Its northernmost reach is Great Point, not nearly so great as it was fifty years ago; the water has nibbled away so much of the soil that it resembles a crippled arm separating Muddy Creek on the east side from Tangier Sound to the west.

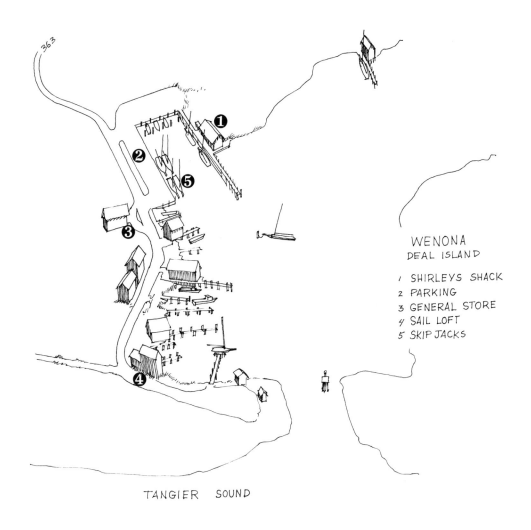

363

① ② ⑤ ③ ④

WENONA
DEAL ISLAND

1 SHIRLEYS SHACK
2 PARKING
3 GENERAL STORE
4 SAIL LOFT
5 SKIPJACKS

TANGIER SOUND

Below Great Point is Cow Point Creek, Fishing Creek, Cedar Island Creek, and Watkins Point, curled upward and off the Maryland-Virginia line by no more than a hundred yards.

Inland, or rather inmarsh, there are Pond Creek, Crooked Creek, The Prong, Cedar Creek, and the only passage navigable by workboats, Broad Creek. The latter has been dredged periodically at great expense so that the scores of workboats sailing to and from Crisfield can move through the marsh, thus saving an extra hour's sail around it. The width of Broad Creek varies from twenty yards to several hundred. Its channel depth can accommodate the heaviest workboat, but stray to port or starboard a short distance in most places and bottom will be discovered quickly.

Cedar Island was for years a gunner's mecca. Enormous rafts of surface-feeding ducks filled its creeks and ponds from fall through winter. (Even in summer, black ducks were populous enough to lure out-of-season hunters into the bug-ridden marsh.) In Pond Creek, redheads were heard pitching in such numbers that their "meowing" would keep the sleepiest hunter wide awake.

The canvasback, the most sought after of all the ducks, was prevalent for some years. Market gunners, with their lethal homemade punt guns, camouflaged skiffs, and entrancing bow lights, killed hundreds of thousands of the birds for profitable sale to restaurants as far north as New York City. One fanciful account of how the canvasback got its name apparently originated in Crisfield. The ducks were stuffed inside wooden barrels, a measure of crushed ice was thrown on top, and across the barrel mouths were stretched squares of canvas, which were tacked down tightly. The cloth was expensive and the packers made known their intentions to recycle the fabric by printing on each barrel the words "Please send canvas back."

Few hunters bother to trek through Cedar Island Marsh any more. The ducks are nearly all gone; their numbers have been greatly thinned for a number of reasons. Some say they were overhunted; others claim early attempts to control the mosquito population by draining the marshes killed the specific plants upon which the waterfowl feed; and still others hold that their breeding grounds have been destroyed. Cedar Island Marsh, in a sense, is little known today but to the few crabbers and muskrat trappers who use it because it is close to town, even though the crabs and 'rats there are not abundant. Excepting Broad Creek, heavy workboats cannot be taken into the island's waters. Only light, simple skiffs powered by small outboards can make it into the shallows; when the tide is out, the skiff must be propelled over the soft bottom manually with a long pole.

West of Crisfield, across the ten miles of Tangier Sound, rises quaggy, sea-saturated Smith Island. On days when the Sound is not cloaked in fog or obscured with its own steamy haze, Smith Island can be seen from the mainland as a long sliver of brownish green floating on its vaporish reflection. At night, and again only when the air is clear, a sprinkle of blinking electric lights from the island villages is visible.

Smith Island, Maryland's only year-round inhabited island not connected by bridge to mainland, actually is an archipelago of marshes and hummocks. Prairie-flat and prickling with pine stands, the island is rife with guts, coves, and thoroughfares. In many places the land is barely a foot above Bay level, and the water, except where the channels are dredged for navigation, is barely a foot deep. Sailors not familiar with the island's waterways or too trusting of its channel markers (winter ice can shift them considerably) often steer their boats onto the soft bottom. It is a common sight in summer—small motor-powered boats pulling sailboats off the mud and back into the deeper water.

It is very likely that Smith Island and Tangier Island, its Virginia counterpart several miles to the south, were once a single island more than fifteen miles in length and six or seven in width. The water now separating the islands is shallow; at low tide most of it is not passable except by skiff or canoe. The submerged land probably was at least a marsh linking the two larger masses before wind and wave worked them asunder.

By most accounts Smith Island was named for the English explorer and cartographer Captain John Smith, whose flattering description of the lower Chesapeake is the single most repeated collection of words in the Bay's public relations history. ". . . Heaven and earth never agreed better to frame a place for man's inhabitation . . . ," Smith wrote in a log he kept during a ten-week exploration of the region. It is not commonly known whether Smith made the observation before or after his experiences with the squalls, the dagger-tailed rays, and the Indians who on at least one occasion forced him to be their guest.

Regardless, Smith and his crew were the first Europeans to chart the waters and map the coastline of the entire Chesapeake Bay using data gotten through personal experience. Smith's map, entitled "Virginia," served as the prototype of all other Bay maps for six decades afterwards.

Near Tylerton, Smith Island

Smith named the group of islands in that vicinity the Russel Isles after his companion and physician who had sailed the Atlantic with him to the New World. Not until three decades later did Smith's name become attached to the islands.

Smith Island has been inhabited for three centuries predominantly by families with a British heritage. Most of the five hundred or so residents (the population has dropped by more than a half within the last century, in part due to an unpredictable seafood industry and to the lure of more stable work on the mainland) claim direct descendancy from the original Evans, Tyler, Bradshaw, and Whitelock settlers. The names inscribed on the churchyard burial markers are the names of those on the island post office rolls.

Captain Johnny Whitelock's forty-eight-foot *Island Belle* was more practical than pretty when she first crossed Tangier Sound from Smith Island to Crisfield's barrel wharf. She had a high bow and a swooping deck much like that on a buy boat. Directly behind the main cabin was a large enclosed room where passengers huddled against the stacked freight when the wind was cold and wet; on the roof, railed on all four sides, more provisions were stacked and when the sky was blue and unthreatening, young passengers clambered about high above the water.

GREEN INSIDE CABIN.

RUST

For fifty-eight years, longer than the lifespan of the average waterman when she was built, the *Belle* sailed back and forth over the Sound, ferrying mail, food, passengers, furniture, cases of soda, mountains of soft crab boxes, radios and later television sets, and occasionally a partially hidden case of beer or a bottle of whiskey tucked somewhere out of sight.

Clocks could be set by the *Belle*'s arrivals and departures from Crisfield. Occasionally, however, she made an unscheduled trip from her island berth to the mainland. In the evening, her bow light on the horizon could mean that someone was ill and in need of a doctor, or that a woman was about to give birth, or that there was a delivery for a Crisfield undertaker.

The *Belle* was retired from service in the late 1970s, and she soon lay half-submerged at her moorings in the busy channel along Tylerton, the southernmost village on Smith Island. The *Belle* is not the only derelict vessel in the creek. There are always a few nosed onto the shoreline awaiting repairs that never seem to be made. But the *Belle*'s condition disturbed many of the islanders. Attempts to patch the holes in her hull and refloat her as a sort of monument to island life have been unsuccessful, even though she has been listed in the National Historic Register as an historic vessel.

More modern island ferries, none as long as the *Belle* and all lighter and faster, now make her daily run to the mainland in the morning, back to the island at noon, and then the same route again. Their wake washes against the *Belle* as they motor in and out of Tylerton.

Three small villages contain the entire island population. Ewell and Tylerton are accessible to each other by boat; Rhodes Point, formerly Rogues Point, is situated on the western side of the island on slightly higher terrain. It and Ewell are connected by a mile of road first paved by the townspeople themselves in 1937. Automobiles are of little practical importance on the island. Yet there are a few cars and pickup trucks which are driven for diversion or are used to carry crab pots from house to shanty or to take an invalid member of a family to visit friends or to go to church. None of the vehicles carry current tags, since they are exempt under state law. Most are older models and probably would not pass inspection for use on mainland roads. Carried to the island on the fuel transport out of Crisfield, the cars and pickups generally are driven until they break down. When this happens, they are left where they stopped running, or they are towed to a sandy landfill and added to a mountain of rusting hulks which has become the greatest eyesore in the island's panoply of nature. On at least one occasion government helicopters were summoned to airlift the wrecks from Smith to another, uninhabited island where they were used to form an elementary type of erosion control. Television stations on the western shore, alerted of the cleanup operation, came to the island to film the spectacle. For some metropolitan viewers of the evening news, it was the first introduction to the little island near the mouth of the Bay. For others, it was a sign that even the quaint and bucolic islanders share some of the problems of mainland cities.

The busiest part of each town is the waterfront, except on Sunday when the island's three churches are filled with congregation and hymn (although not at the same time, since the one Methodist preacher must go from one church to the other conducting separate services). Ewell, Tylerton, and Rhodes Point survive on the bounty of the Bay, so it is along the docks and piers that the people gather each day, loading and unloading the catches, tinkering with mechanical devices, and conversing loudly from one boat slip to another. Despite the five thousand tourists who come to the island each year, the tourist trade so far is relatively unexploited. The small groups of visitors who come by ferry from the western shore to Rhodes Point and from Crisfield to Ewell and Tylerton make little more racket than that raised by low chatter and the clicking of camera shutters.

Day's End, Tilghman Island

Projecting out to the channel from the bulk-headed shoreline along each town are piers in various degrees of stability. One-room sheds and crab houses, some painted white and others—clearly the majority—weathered grey, stand poised above the shallow water. Below, on the soft bottom, assortments of metal and wooden objects are the dull brown of sediment. Tin cans, engine parts, bushel baskets with broken slats and without bottoms, and plastic bottles are cluttered about.

When not being steered around the island or out in the Sound in search of a catch, dozens of workboats are tied up at the piers. As elsewhere on the Shore, fiberglass hulls are becoming more popular; most of the wood-hulled workboats are at least ten years old. Even less visible on the Bay are the drake-tailed workboats. Most of these can be seen on Smith Island, and the style has come to be associated entirely with this area. The stern of the boat is tapered into the water, resembling the rear section of a sea duck as it swims along the surface.

This peculiar but graceful contour stabilizes the boat on rough seas, a characteristic especially useful while navigating along a line of crab pots in a blustery wind. The major drawback of the design is that its somewhat complicated construction requires more upkeep than the standard flush stern.

The channels of the dredged thoroughfares by the towns are not much more than fifty or sixty feet wide in many places. On the far sides, opposite the piers, are more pierlike erections, unattached to the shoreline and supporting large crab houses and holding tanks where crabs are "fished up" soon after shedding their shells. The crabs, delicate but feisty, are cleaned—their eyes and lungs are cut away—and packed in cool seaweed-filled waxed cartons to be shipped across the Sound to the refrigerated trucks waiting in Crisfield.

All around these offshore piers are pine poles driven into the mud, outlining what were rectangular corrals or pens. Wide planks were nailed horizontally from stake to stake to make walls against the wave actions that could swamp the crab-filled floats

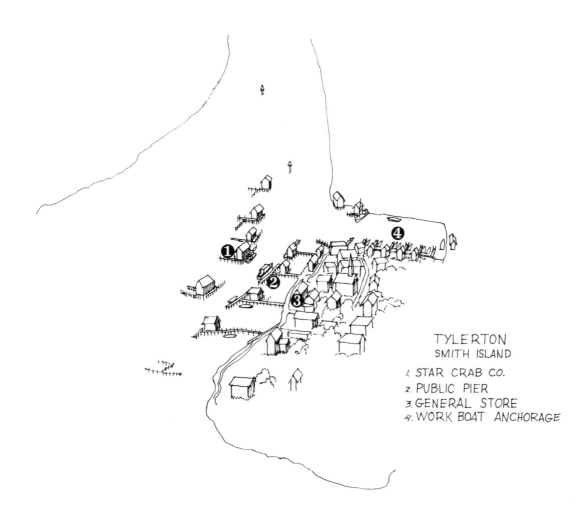

TYLERTON
SMITH ISLAND

1. STAR CRAB CO.
2. PUBLIC PIER
3. GENERAL STORE
4. WORK BOAT ANCHORAGE

once used to contain the shedder crabs. The crabber had to pole his skiff about the floats, watching closely for the crabs which had just shed and lifting them out before their new shells began to harden. Now that pumps keep water flowing through the holding tanks built on the piers, the soft crabs can be harvested more efficiently. The outdated latticed floats lie on the marsh banks; each year a few more fall apart or are taken to the mainland by relic-seekers and restaurant owners who use them to decorate dining rooms.

The whole arrangement of piers jutting off the shore and crab houses lining the other side of the channel create a watery boulevard, the most traveled street in town.

Daytrippers taking the noon passenger boats out of Crisfield find that they are not pressed for time while on the island. The regular ferry stops in Ewell and Tylerton offer the foot traveler a leisurely paced stroll along the waterfronts and down the short, narrow streets past houses with small yards enclosed with picket fences. (Those islanders who live on the fringe of town have rather larger backyards—acres upon acres of marshland.) There are a few single-story houses, sided in aluminum. But the majority of homes are turn-of-the-century wooden structures with two floors and concrete foundations. Naturally, none of the buildings has a basement; the water table is so high that in the crowded churchyards caskets are not actually buried, but sealed in concrete vaults set but a few inches into the earth.

The clowder of cats on Smith Island appears to be larger in number than might be expected (if one were inclined to even think about the issue). With the surrounding water rather imposing a limit to their search for marsh mice and with the highest land being that upon which the towns have been built, the cats tend to spend most of their time wandering about yards and casually crossing the few streets there are to cross.

The cats seem content enough, unbothered and certainly not starving. But all are not cared for by single families, since many of the cats must think it the duty of the entire town to look out for their comfort and survival. For example, a cat given away in Tylerton to another family may be taken no more than a street's distance away. And on Smith Island, it is difficult to drop a cat off in the country; it might very well be in a neighbor's yard.

A pedestrian is not apt to trip over a cat, yet cats are nearly everywhere. They are peeking around corner foundations, stalking, walking territorially along fences, and crouching on sun-warmed cement steps. They languish with an air of caprice.

The drama of exile on Smith Island is not as great today as it was but a few decades ago. There is no airport on the island because any proposals to build one have been rejected. Helicopters, however, are able to drop food and fuel when the Bay freezes and icebreakers are unable to cut through Tangier Sound. When an emergency medical situation arises, again helicopters can carry out individuals to a landing pad built onto the hospital in Crisfield.

The island boats are faster than they have ever been. It requires very little effort for an islander to make several trips to and from the mainland in a single day. The number of tourists is increasing, so contact with the world beyond the island's marshy fringes is greater than ever before.

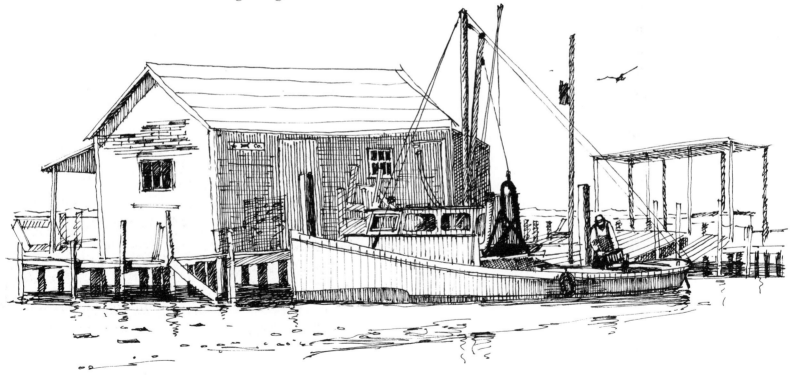

Smith Island's natural aloofness has caused concern in the past. During the winter of 1918 when the waters around Smith were thick with ice, state newspapers were giving front-page service to the islanders' predicament. No one had heard from the island in four weeks when a group of men huddled in a Crisfield shop and related the trials they had undergone to reach the harbor. Eleven of them took off from the island across the ice, pulling a boat until they reached the open waters in the deepest part of Tangier Sound. When they struck ice again, they pulled the boat for four more miles in a snowstorm until they reached Crisfield. Smith's inhabitants, they said, were out of fuel and the only food available was a pasty meal of flour and gravy.

Smith Islanders were not as fortunate as those living on Holland Island a couple miles to the northwest. After the ice had melted enough to allow boats on the water, several watermen heard gunshots coming from Holland. Thinking the volleys were signals for help, the sailors hurried to reach the island, only to discover upon reaching the shore that the residents were merely preparing their daily dinner of wild duck. When the freeze came, it stranded rafts of waterfowl on Holland, easily enough to keep the islanders in meat until the spring thaw.

(Holland Islanders fared less well later that same year in the flu epidemic that swept the coast. Many residents became ill and died. The survivors packed their belongings, actually took apart their homes, and moved onto the Shore. Along Crisfield's main street several of the Holland Island houses were reconstructed; they remain there today. Only one building remains on Holland Island, and it is occupied usually only during ducking season. The island itself is but a portion of its original size. Most of it has been washed into the Bay.)

On another occasion, eighteen winters later, Smith Islanders shared the suffering when again ice made the crossing to Crisfield nearly impossible. An expectant woman became very ill. She was bundled aboard the *Belle* and, with a number of volunteers on hand, the mail boat started out for the mainland. Thick ice stretched across Tangier

Sound. The men gathered at the boat's bow and took turns breaking the ice with their feet. The *Belle* moved so slowly at times that her engine was almost at an idle. The trip that normally took two hours lasted ten that day. The woman lost her child when the group finally reached Crisfield; a Coast Guard cutter made a path through the ice for the *Belle* as she returned to the island carrying the infant for burial.

Smith Island has never been figuratively more close to Crisfield than now. Island watermen bring their crabs and oysters to the Crisfield market, island teenagers attend high school in Crisfield, and there are as many islanders working in Crisfield as there are Crisfielders married and living on the island. On any day, the passengers on the island ferries having business or social relationships with islanders outnumber tourists.

Yet Smith Islanders retain a sense of independence not only from Crisfield, but from the rest of the Shore and from the entire state. All three towns have shunned the minibureaucracies that accompany incorporation, unlike many communities on the Shore. There is no formal government apparatus outside the church. While Crisfield is as wet as any Shore town, Smith Island is, on the surface, as dry as a sun-baked oyster shell. (To be sure, the girth of some of the islanders is not solely the result of too much cake and pie. Watermen drink quite openly, often without restraint, in Crisfield bars. But back on the island beer and whiskey are kept out of sight. Tippling tourists are looked upon with a stern Methodist eye.)

Despite annual protestations by state health officials, many Smith Island women continue to pick and package crab meat for sale on the mainland. By law, Maryland crab meat intended for commercial use must be processed, handled, and packed by licensed facilities. Nevertheless, hundreds of pounds of crab meat are carried from island kitchens across Tangier Sound to Crisfield each summer. In most instances, it is the best priced, most shell-free, tastiest crab meat on the Bay.

MISS EVANS

JAMES DRAKE IAMS A.W.S. '80

Duck hunting on the island has dropped considerably, as it has elsewhere on the Shore. But it takes little effort—a phone call or two—to have a duck delivered from the island to the Crisfield dock.

GAS CAN
BY THE
FEET

FISHING CREEK

Notes on the Paintings

Because I hope that a large part of the audience for this book will be painters, and because I have been a teacher all of my adult life—and still am—I cannot help relating some of the circumstances and sharing some of the watercolor techniques used in the creation of the paintings reproduced in this book. My comments are very informal. My hope is to encourage people to visit this area, look, sketch, paint—and have as good a time as I have had in the process.

—James Drake Iams

Hubbard's Dock, Rock Hall

This crab company warehouse painting is a composite watercolor. The workboat, for example, was taken from a previous sketch and placed into the composition, as were the figures, to make the painting more interesting. Similarly, the sky has been created to establish a particular mood. Its unusual coloring suggests late afternoon.

After the painting was dry, the side of *Mary Ann*, the workboat, was burnished with a glass marble. This smoothed out the rough texture of the watercolor paper, and eliminated the minute shadows that are cast by the texture, giving the white area a brilliance that the natural roughness of the paper would otherwise tend to soften.

Oyster Tonger, Fishing Creek, Hooper Island

The effect of snow in this painting was achieved by spraying liquid frisket on the watercolor paper, after roughing in the drawing and before wetting and painting the surface. The background was painted by using diagonal strokes to indicate the direction from which the snow was falling. I'll describe more about this later.

Tonging is practiced all through the area and it is a good painting subject, especially since it presents an opportunity to capture a person in action. Watch for the authenticity of detail, of course, both in the activity of the waterman and in his boat and gear.

Break Time, Tilghman Island

The watermen of the Chesapeake Bay, wearing their fertilizer hats, are interesting studies. One must sketch quickly. They are constantly working, constantly on the move, unloading their catch or motoring to and from the pier in their workboats.

This healthy looking company man was sketched while taking a break from unloading oysters on a pier at Knapps Narrows.

Color tone washes were first applied to the painting followed by shadows and, finally, details. A color tone is a wash using the local color in its lightest and brightest form. A darkening of this same tone will create the shadow value. The gray-blue parts were darkened several times to create a strong light and dark pattern against the baskets of oysters.

Wanting to concentrate entirely on the figure, I eliminated all of the background without even pretending to put in fog or mist. This treatment of a subject, floating in white space, is called a vignette, and gives the finished painting the spontaneous character of a sketch.

Tilghman is a nice place to paint.

Angler's Marina, Kent Narrows

Angler's Marina and Bar was sketched at Kent Narrows from a pier by the Yacht Club which lies on the west side of the narrows. The building, the gas and seafood bar signs, the piers, and the overall clutter make an interesting arrangement for a painting and give the scene a character of its own. Sometimes you want to concentrate the viewer's attention on one carefully selected subject, and you do this by eliminating the background, omitting things that are really there but that would be distracting if you kept them in your painting, as if to magnify your subject. Here, though, the opposite is true. I don't want to eliminate anything to simplify the painting; I want to include everything. Notice that there are not only the things I have just mentioned, but also cars in the parking lot, a "diving" signal flag, flying incongruously from a building, pilings, boats—the bustle of myriad elements.

Shipping Creek, Kent Island

This quiet, lazy cove lies on the southern part of Kent Island and harbors these stark, white workboats silhouetted here against the multicolored trees on the far shore. Seagulls and

Chesapeake Bay workboats all face into the wind when at rest.

The painting was done on prestretched 140-pound Saunders watercolor paper. There are several ways of stretching the paper, but my technique is to soak it for about twenty minutes in a bathtub. I then place it on a drawing board and fasten it down with staples about every 2 inches apart around the edges. Some artists use masking tape all around; instead of a board, some use the stretchers designed for canvas for oil painting. But whatever is used, and however the paper is fastened, what the process does is roughly equivalent to preshrinking a fabric. The stretched paper, tacked down all around, shrinks and becomes very taut as it dries, making it a marvelous surface to work on. More importantly, however, it keeps the paper from absorbing uneven amounts of water as you paint on it, which would cause the paper to stretch or expand irregularly. A painting done on unstretched paper does not—it cannot—dry flat.

When the painting is completed, the matting covers the staple marks and the viewer never sees them. A watercolor block is essentially a pad of prestretched paper, with the paper padded or "bound" on all four sides.

Morning Coffee, Oxford

I found this well-kept sloop behind Cutts & Case, Wiley Shipyard in Oxford. Having sailed the Chesapeake Bay for twenty years, I have seen many a sloop in the water. This is one of the more beautiful ones that I had seen, and I couldn't resist making a painting of her.

It is essential, in my opinion, that the painter understand the subject before painting it. If you are painting and are in doubt as to a detail, I suggest you get up from your little camp stool and, if possible, study the subject at close range. Sometimes it pays to look at the subject from

different angles. The more you understand about what you are seeing, the better you can portray the very essence of your subject.

One of the nice things about sailing, or certainly one of the things I enjoyed most, is being able to get up in the early morning, sit in the cockpit under a canopy, and have yourself a nice hot cup of coffee. Few things are more pleasant. Nostalgically, because of this, I created the two figures and put them in the cockpit of this sloop, having their morning coffee. In order to emphasize the boat and the lines of the boat and the beauty of it, I chose to eliminate the background. Although in fact there was a clutter of masts and rigging in the background, I made an early morning haze or fog hanging over the water, eliminating all those distractions.

Knapps Narrows, Tilghman Island

This is a panoramic view of the Knapps Narrows—the waterway separating Tilghman Island from the mainland. In the distance you can see the drawbridge over the narrows.

Notice that the posts and some of the rocks in the foreground are pure white. These were masked out by the use of liquid frisket before the painting got started. Let me tell you about it.

Liquid frisket is a soft gummy substance, usually gray or sometimes orange, that you can apply with a brush. Just like the wax in a batik, this frisket protects the paper from what goes on over it and, when it is removed (after the painting is completed), the paper it has protected is unblemished.

In order to apply a frisket correctly, you should first put your brush into water and work it into soap before dipping into the liquid frisket. The soap in the brush will help you clean the brush later. Getting dried frisket out of a brush that has not been soaped is almost impossible. (Repeat the process each time you dip into the frisket.)

First the scene is sketched. Then the liquid frisket is used to protect those little areas you want to keep perfectly white. When the frisket is dry, proceed with the painting. At the very end, after the painting is thoroughly dried, the frisket is removed with the use of a little ball of dried rubber cement that architects call a "mouse." This lifts the frisket off the paper completely. Although the side of the cabin of the boat is also dead white, frisket was not used there. In small areas, the frisket works beautifully, but in large, broad areas it is apt—when removed—to tear up the paper a bit and ruin its surface. That is very unattractive. It is best, in large areas such as this, to paint around them.

Several things are prominent on the Eastern Shore—workboats, skipjacks, crabs, oysters, and pickup trucks. This orange pickup truck was really there when I sketched, so I didn't have to invent it. Its orange happily complements the green in the painting. The mooring lines on the white boat were rendered with gouache, or opaque watercolor.

Anna McGarvey, Tilghman Island

In order to capture the high contrast of the white hull of the *Anna McGarvey* against the warm, green grass and dark water of the narrows, I stood on the bank at low tide to make a sketch. This perspective allowed me to have a composition stressing the bowsprit of the freshly painted skipjack. The lines and shrouds and mooring lines are authentic and are essential elements of the finished watercolor. A ruler is a great aid in rendering standing rigging. Standing rigging is the rigging that supports the masts of boats. Side supports are called shrouds; fore and aft ones

are forestays and backstays. They are usually taut. Running rigging, on the other hand, is the rigging that controls the sails and, certainly when sails are down, are usually limp. They can be done freehand but must be accurate. In order to put in the running rigging, I often put my paint brush down at one end of where the line is, look to where it is going to go, give a little prayer, and go at it. Since, by this time in the painting, you have laid in the sky and the background, you have only one chance to do this and do it correctly.

When painting water on the spot, I find that closing my eyes and "photographing" it in my mind, and then proceeding with the sketch, is a very effective technique. It lets the image rest a moment in my mind and then lets me sketch what I remember. I find that if you sit there and watch the water ripple, ripple, ripple, you can become very confused.

Applegarth's Pier, Oxford

I am sometimes asked what I take with me when I go out to sketch—how I go about it. My equipment consists of a little camp stool, a sketching tablet, and a felt tip pen, either water soluble or not. The sketch for this particular painting was done with a water soluble felt tip, and I was thus able to moisten my fingers and rub over the ink to give a bit of tone here and there.

I find it best, as I enter a boatyard or a place where I want to paint, to look up someone in authority and ask permission to be there. I tell him or her what I plan to do and have never encountered any problems. I suspect, though, that anyone walking around with a sketch tablet and a folding camp stool would be able to go practically anywhere without being challenged.

This sketch was done in the early morning. I like to paint or sketch in the early morning because of the shadows that occur in the early hours. At noon there aren't very interesting dark and light patterns, but early morning or late afternoon is good, with the light streaming across your subjects.

Once the sketch is complete, and I think I have everything that I need to make the painting, I usually also take a picture. I use a 35-millimeter camera and color slide film. When it comes to making the painting I refer not only to my sketch but also to the slide for any details that I might have overlooked. I project the slide from the rear onto a piece of ground glass that I mount at the top of my easel, and this makes me feel as if I am almost back on the spot. The scene is right in front of me as clearly and as brightly as it had been when I was sitting there sketching it. When the painting is being done several months after the sketch, this reminder is frequently a big help.

This painting exemplifies another technical detail also, and this relates to the standing rigging on the boats in the background. These lines are put in with a knife. After the painting is essentially done, and the paper is still wet, you put in these lines with the point of a knife blade. If you "wipe" the line, scraping the pigment off as you go, almost as you might spread butter, the line will remain light in color. If, on the other hand, you gouge the line by scoring, or even very lightly cutting the paper, the pigment from the surrounding area will gather in that cut and the line will then be dark when it dries. This is pretty tricky, but it works beautifully after you have practiced it a bit.

Cherry Street, St. Michaels

Here is one of the many picturesque houses in St. Michaels, and this gives me a chance to talk a little about shadows. Along with highlighted areas, shadows tell you a great deal about the

structure of things. Often the viewer learns about the shape of an object not only from the way the artist draws it, but also from the shadows it casts. Often, for example, we will paint an object coming toward us. When it is foreshortened, it is sometimes difficult to see its true form, and yet if it casts a shadow onto a flat surface, its form can be revealed. The shadow helps describe it. In this painting we can see that the porches come out to the roof line, but that the house does not—and the reason we know this is that the walls of the house, behind the porches, are in deep shadow.

About windows: there are no shortcuts. Each pane of glass must be painted with thought and care even though, in a colonial building for example, with many windows and many panes in each of them, this can be a pretty boring process. The same is true of such things as the carpentry on the porch in this picture—the little intricate Victorian woodwork must be rendered as carefully and in as much detail as possible—all with a spirit of freedom, however, which retains the water color "feel" in the painting.

Converted Buy Boat, Cambridge

This old buy boat, tied up at the Cambridge inlet, caught my eye. I painted it on hot press paper.

Hot press paper, as it is being made and after the sheet has been formed, is pressed between heated metal plates to give it a very hard, smooth surface. This smooth paper tends to brighten the finished watercolor because there is no "tooth," or texture, to the surface of the paper. Light cast upon it will not cast any shadows and thus the whiteness of the paper is very, very white. A watercolor done on this smooth, white paper is much brighter than it would be on a textured sheet. I did the painting with a round ferrule brush, number 6. It permits you to paint smaller areas, but it almost requires you to work in a slower fashion, and to give a little more delicacy to the painting. Because the brush will hold less water (and thus less color pigment), the strokes are small and one must go back and paint areas more than once in order to build the value-contrast between one subject, in one area, and another. The final effect is English in its style. English painters used to work delicately in the field, on the spot, with a round ferrule brush, to create and capture the color tones of the scene at the moment—and later would go back and do a finished painting. This little painting, then, rendered with a small brush on smooth paper, gives the feeling of a quickly done watercolor sketch, the feeling of a study done in preparation for a larger, more ambitious painting.

Reflections, St. Michaels

From one side of the little inner harbor at St. Michaels, you can look across and see this board-and-batten building and the pier and the boats reflected in the still water. Let me make more observations about shadows and reflections.

Notice how shadows, especially on the buildings, are a major way of showing a third dimension. The shadow under the eaves of the yellow house, for example, add a very real feeling of depth. The shadow under the eaves of the shed give a third dimension to the board and batten structure even though it is, relatively speaking, flat.

Unless the sun is directly overhead, shadows are going to fall to the left or to the right, or backwards or forwards—but reflections always come directly toward you.

In painting ripples on water, a basic rule to follow is to remember that the trough of a wave is always lighter than the top or crest of the wave. Many artists reverse this procedure and then wonder what is wrong with the water.

Blackwater

There are few places on the Eastern Shore that can compare with Blackwater National Wildlife Refuge in the late fall, if you want to "capture" ducks, geese, and even bald eagles. You can find all the subject matter for painting these birds that you will ever want to find.

In this particular case, the painting was done from some slides taken at Blackwater. I have found that, to portray birds in flight, you either have to photograph them, using a telephoto lens—arresting their motion on a slide—or you must sit there for several hours studying the birds in flight, closing your eyes, remembering what you have seen, and then sketching from this visual image (rather than from the birds themselves). I mentioned this technique earlier, when I was talking about painting active water, and the reason is the same. When something is constantly in motion, you must stop looking for a moment in order to "see" what you have seen.

Meekins Neck

To the west of the road leading to Hooper Island, this scene appears time and again. The workboat, nesting in the channel among the dead marsh grass, and the long, flat horizon line, are typical on the lower Eastern Shore.

Keeping the horizon line low in the composition stresses the "table-top" flatness of the terrain, but it is the sky that sets the mood for the painting. Let me describe how I go about painting a sky like this. I first wet the surface of the paper—rather abundantly—and then, working into the damp area, I lay on the color and let it "bleed." The wetness of the paper, by a kind of capillary attraction, makes the pigment spread irregularly and creates soft, feathery edges to the clouds—and a feeling of cloud movement. I must be careful to let this dry completely before working over or next to the sky area.

Back Creek, Hooper Island

The tires dropped over stakes to serve as bumpers struck me as an inventive way of using old tires. As unattractive and junky as an empty beer can, the scene still attracted me. The painting was done primarily with transparent colors, but the dead marsh grass in the foreground was rendered with opaque gouache. Opaque, warm colors tend to establish the foreground, helping to give the painting a sense of depth. The mallards, very common around such an area, were added.

Crocheron

This painting of the old shanty and staked out row-boats down at Crocheron was painted on hot press paper. As I have mentioned before, it does not absorb the paint as readily as a rougher paper, and this permits me to go back into the painting and lay in additional washes over already-washed-in areas. This is very similar to glazing an oil painting where, to darken an area, for example, one mixes a very thin solution of color and then washes over the existing paint to tint it darker. The underlying paint, of course, has to be dry. You will find that with hot press paper you almost *have* to glaze in over existing areas to get the depth and the darkness that you want. The sky in the painting was painted while the surface was wet, but the top was much wetter than the middle. As I worked toward the horizon line you can see where the paper was drier since the paint has more of a hard edge than it does at the top of the painting.

Evening, Deal Island

This little scene is on the far side of Shirley's Shack. Off in the distance there were a couple of little shanties and two skipjacks tied up. When I see something like this, I jump on it like a dog onto raw meat. I love to do this sort of thing. It's so typically Eastern Shore. There are a lot of little piers that kind of dance up and down across the water and I can't resist. Here again the horizon is kept low. The serenity of the scene was helped further by limiting my palette to the minimum. The painting was done quickly and was kept very simple—much the way you might render something in preparation for a larger, more complicated canvas. Often the simplest statement is the best statement.

Waterfront, Crisfield

I think the most striking thing about this scene was the late afternoon sky and the way the warm light flooded the facades of all the buildings facing the waters of Tangier Sound. The boat in the foreground and the waterman add a little animation to the painting. The composition is often what I refer to as an "L composition," which is a very safe one. I particularly liked the strong dark and light patterns on the buildings—all those vertical, repeated lines. This scene is looking north from the public pier, and it represents an unusual opportunity to view a row of buildings as if from out on the water.

Skipjack, Deal Island

On this particular day, across the harbor toward Shirley's Shack, there were three skipjacks tied, all being worked on. The watermen were getting ready to go out and dredge and redistribute seed oysters and thus were putting new plywood on the decks to help hold the load of shells that they were going to dredge.

I chose one of the three to paint. What I wanted to bring out in the picture, of course, was both the old skipjack in need of repair, and its rigging. It was done in my studio from a sketch

which I had made in my sketch book. This let me do something you can't do in the field, and that is to use a hair dryer to dry large surfaces, such as the sky, so that I could more quickly move on into the rest of the painting. It saves a lot of time. The paper has to be bone dry before anything can be laid in over it—in this case, the rigging—and the hair dryer let me do it almost right away rather than to set the painting aside overnight. I used a ruler here, incidentally, to help me put in the standing rigging.

Near Tylerton, Smith Island

In this composition I've stressed the horizontal feeling to the Eastern Shore by lengthening the format in relation to its height.

This painting gives me a chance to comment on some other points. You'll notice that the blacks in the painting have been picked up—repeated—in several places. They're under the sluffing pens of the peeler floats, under the fishing shack, in the abandoned pier or pilings in the right background, and in the Mercury motor on the boat in the foreground. This repetition of a sharp accent isn't necessarily noticed, but it helps unify the painting. I've also taken an artist's liberty here. The telephone pole, in the sketch that I did, is right smack in the middle, dividing the composition in two. I moved it to the right when I did the painting. It looks natural enough, so I haven't violated anything—and the composition is much improved.

Day's End, Tilghman Island

I mentioned earlier how essential I think it is to understand what one is painting, and that is demonstrated in this picture. Notice how the bow of this boat rises and how low it is at the stern. This difference is referred to as the shear of the boat, and the shear of the Eastern Shore workboat can be as much as two or three feet. I think it is safe to say that no two of these boats are exactly alike, but there are a number of things that seem to typify the Eastern Shore workboat—the little cuddycabin up front, the canopy over the cockpit and the stakes that hold it up, the engine box, the bait box, the bushel baskets that hold the crabs, the mufflered exhaust pipe standing up next to the engine, and so forth. The little red knobs at the gunwale on the right of the engine box are the motor controls, and the stick—the vertical level which is highlighted in the darkness of the companionway—is the steering mechanism. The captain of the boat can stand there and by pushing the stick forward, steer the boat to the right, and by pulling it back, to the left. He can work his trotline simply by standing in one position. He controls both speed and direction of his boat and works his trotline at the same time. The diagonal braces out of the stern are attached to a settling board, which keeps the boat from "digging in" while under way. If a boat doesn't sit down, doesn't dig in, it won't displace so much water, and therefore won't use as much fuel.

Star Crab Company, Smith Island

I was attracted to this scene, as any artist would be, I'm sure, by the rebus Star Crab Company sign. Tied up there is a patent tonger, a waterman cleaning up after a day's catch.

The white foam in the water in the foreground was masked out with liquid frisket, as were the booms on the *Miss Evans*.

The important thing in a painting such as this is patience. In this instance, the siding on the building simply has to be painted with meticulous care or it will not look right. This is how I went about it.

The local color on the sunny side of the fishing shack was painted first, allowed to dry, and then (using a ruler and a small striper brush) I painted in the lines between the bricks. These, of course, are not real bricks, but an asphalt siding simulating bricks, but from a painter's point of view they might as well be real and you have to render them as if they were. After I striped in the lines between the bricks, I then used a quarter-inch brush and, a single stroke at a time, painted in the darker bricks that appear in a random pattern on the side of the building. Then I tackled the shaded side of the shack, using a darker local color, repeating the procedure I have just described. Proper perspective has to be observed.

Putting the red shirt on the man who is unloading baskets of crabs is a stunt I have borrowed from John Constable. In his landscapes he always had a little boy with a red jacket or a little red cap, and I thought that the touch of red here would be a nice way to spotlight the figure.

Materials and Equipment

Each individual painter will have favorites with respect to papers, brushes, and palette. Here is what I use for painting watercolors.

Papers:

Saunders, 140 lb. block or stretched.
Arches, 140 lb. hotpress, block or stretched.
Bockingford, 140 lb. block or stretched.
Fabriano Cold Press.

Brushes:

1 in. Single stroke (flat)
½ in. Single stroke (flat)
¼ in. Single stroke (flat)
⅛ in. Single stroke (flat)
#6 round
#3 round
#0 striper

Colors:

Transparent
Cadmium Yellow
Cadmium Yellow Deep
Yellow Ochre
Cadmium Orange
Winsor Red
Light Red
Burnt Sienna
Warm Sepia
Burnt Umber
Winsor Green
Oxide of Chromium

Cerulean Blue
Prussian Blue
Cobalt Blue
Neutral Tint
Lamp Black
Designers Gouache
Zinc White
Golden Yellow
Yellow Ochre
Cadmium Orange
Burnt Sienna
Ivory Black

Liquid Frisket or Mask

Bayside Impressions

MARYLAND'S EASTERN SHORE AND THE CHESAPEAKE BAY

has been composed by the publisher in Mergenthaler's Linoterm Caledonia. The type used for the title is Photo-Lettering York. Color separations were prepared by Capper, Incorporated, Knoxville, Tennessee. Printed and bound by Kingsport Press, Kingsport, Tennessee.

TIDEWATER PUBLISHERS

Centreville, Maryland

1984